Survival 101 Beginner's Guide 2020: The Complete Guide To Urban And Wilderness Survival

Rory Anderson

Table Of Contents

INTRODUCTION 1

CHAPTER 1 *PREPARING TO SURVIVE* 4

    GAUGING YOUR CURRENT SITUATION 4

    MEASURING EMERGENCY LEVELS 6

    EMERGENCIES YOU ARE MOST LIKELY TO COME ACROSS 8

    PREPARING FOR EXTREME EMERGENCIES 10

    THE SKILLS YOU WILL NEED 11

CHAPTER 2 *KEY TERMS* 13

    AREA OF OPERATION (AO) 13

    A-TEAM 14

    BUG OUT HIDEOUT SITE (BOHS) 15

    EMERGENCY RALLYING POINT (ERP) 15

    GRAB AND GO BAG (GNG BAG) 16

    IMMEDIATE RALLYING POINT (IRP) 17

CHAPTER 3 *THE FIRST FIVE* 19

    THE FIRST FIVE URBAN VS. OFF-GRID ENVIRONMENTS 19

    SHELTER 21

    WATER 24

    FIRE 26

    FOOD 29

    SAFETY 34

CHAPTER 4 *THE TASK LISTS* 37

    TASKS 1 TO 3: PREPARING 37

    TASKS 4 TO 5: ASSESSING 38

    TASKS 6 TO 12: PREVENTION 39

    TASKS 13 TO 14: COMMUNICATION 40

TASKS 15 TO 25: THE FIRST FIVE	41
TASKS 26 TO 27: SPECIAL EQUIPMENT	42
TASK 28 TO 31: EQUIPMENT CHECKLISTS	43
TASKS 32 TO 34: LEAVING	44

CHAPTER 5 *THE 34 TASKS OF SURVIVAL* **45**

TASK 1: A-TEAM CONTACTS	46
TASK 2: WATER BOTTLES	46
TASK 3: FIRST AID KIT	47
TASK 4: CHECK STATUS OF A-TEAM	48
TASK 5: AREA STUDY	49
TASK 6: FIREARM PREVENTION	51
TASK 7: FIRE PREVENTION	51
TASK 8: DROWNING PREVENTION	52
TASK 9: POISON PREVENTION	53
TASK 10: ENVIRONMENTAL DANGER ASSESSMENT AND PREVENTION	55
TASK 11: MAN-MADE DANGER ASSESSMENT AND PREVENTION	56
TASK 12: MAP AND NAVIGATION SUPPLIES	57
TASK 13: EMERGENCY RADIO	58
TASK 14: A-TEAM CODEWORDS	58
TASK 15: ROTATION AND INSPECTION CHECKLIST	60
TASK 16: WATER FOR MILD EMERGENCY	61
TASK 17: WATER FOR MODERATE TO EXTREME EMERGENCY	61
TASK 18: SHELTER FOR MILD EMERGENCY	62
TASK 19: SHELTER FOR MODERATE TO EXTREME EMERGENCY	63
TASK 20: FIRE FOR MILD EMERGENCY	64
TASK 21: FIRE FOR MODERATE TO EXTREME EMERGENCY	65
TASK 22: FOOD FOR MILD EMERGENCY	67
TASK 23: FOOD FOR MODERATE TO EXTREME EMERGENCY	67
TASK 24: FIRST AID FOR MILD EMERGENCY	68
TASK 25: FIRST AID FOR MODERATE TO EXTREME EMERGENCY	69

TASK 26: EMERGENCY EQUIPMENT FOR WORK/SCHOOL 70

TASK 27: DIGITAL COPIES OF IMPORTANT DOCUMENTS 70

TASK 28: TRAVEL EQUIPMENT 70

TASK 29: SURVIVAL VEST EQUIPMENT 71

TASK 30: PERSONAL EQUIPMENT 72

TASK 31: CAR EQUIPMENT 73

TASK 32: PRE-PACKAGED SUPPLIES 73

TASK 33: GNG BAG FOR MILD EMERGENCY 74

TASK 34: GNG BAG FOR MODERATE TO EXTREME EMERGENCY 74

CHAPTER 6 *HOW TO LEAVE AN URBAN ENVIRONMENT* 75

PREPARING YOUR SUPPLIES 75

PLOTTING YOUR DESTINATION 76

EDUCATING YOURSELF ON YOUR DESTINATION 77

LEARNING SKILLS IN ADVANCE 78

SECURING THE FIRST 5 OF SURVIVAL 79

PRACTICE EVACUATIONS 81

CHAPTER 7 *LONG TERM OFF-GRID SURVIVAL* 83

FORAGING AND SCAVENGING IN NATURAL ENVIRONMENTS 83

RAISED BED GARDENING 84

LONG TERM FOOD PRESERVATION 84

PREPARING FOR CLIMATE CHANGES 85

BUILDING LONG TERM SHELTER 85

NAVIGATING DISASTERS 86

CHAPTER 8 *EMERGENCY AND FIRST AID* 88

WHEN TO CONTACT THE POLICE 88

WHEN TO CONTACT FEMA 89

UTILIZING GOVERNMENT INFRASTRUCTURE 89

FIRST AID METHODS YOU SHOULD KNOW 90

DRESSING A WOUND 90

> Treating a Gastrointestinal Illness 91
> Dealing With a Broken Bone 91

CONCLUSION 93
DESCRIPTION 95

INTRODUCTION

None of us could have possibly anticipated the disaster that has come with 2020, nor the state it would leave us in. Between the growing threat of the pandemic and the crashing economy, there is plenty of reason to have doubts about our modern system. Right now is the perfect time to begin developing your survival skills. That way, you'll know exactly how to protect yourself should things get any worse than they already are.

Perhaps the most significant threat we are all facing right now is the growing economic crisis, as well as the pressure it is putting on our current way of life. From a lack of income to messed up supply chains, it is increasingly more challenging to access anything you need for survival these days. While it may not be a big deal that you cannot directly go out and buy new clothes, furniture, and frivolous supplies, it is a growing concern that the strain is reaching deep into our food supplies, our hygienic supplies, and even our access to medications and other health and first aid requirements.

As of right now, there is no clear end in sight, nor is there any plausible solution that seems to be capable of repairing the damage. While many who are in charge continue to spout off about possible ideas and attempt to affirm that everything is fine, it is clear that everything is *not* fine. We don't know how much worse it might get. In an ideal world, we may be able to trust our government to protect us. Still, based on current conditions and experiences, many people are growing rightfully doubtful and distrustful in their government. So, if you cannot trust society, the current state of affairs, supply chains, or your government, what is left for you to do? *Survive.*

We are like any other species when faced with a threat to our very survival. Including the breakdown of our current system, it will all come down to an "every man for himself" situation. This may seem extravagant, but the reality is that hundreds of thousands of people are faced with this every single year. From wildfires, hurricanes, and other natural disasters, to pandemics, economic crashes, and the implementation of police states in some areas, humans have been granted rude awakening after rude awakening. That is that while the current system and connection of supply chains may provide you with convenience and comfort when they are all eliminated, you are left with *nothing*. If you don't know how to survive without them, the minute an emergency arises, you will find yourself staring down a serious threat and having no idea what to do about it. Only those who educate themselves will survive the deadliest of emergencies. If you want to be one of them, you have to take your education seriously.

Survival 101: Beginner's Guide 2020 will help you navigate our current state of affairs. It is also designed to help you navigate *any* state of crisis. Whether the emergency is mild, moderate, or extreme, you will discover everything you need to know. Please note that while this book will support hobbyists who want to prepare for the future, this book is certainly not geared toward hobbyists. This book is designed to help in real-life emergency survival situations. Everything you will discover in this book will tell you precisely what you need to do to survive any crisis you happen across.

While much of this book is written specifically for the purpose of surviving in a natural environment, I realize that you might currently be residing in an urban setting. For that reason, there will be information on urban survival and escaping urban situations as needed, should you find yourself in that situation. Please be sure to educate yourself based on your current circumstances so that you can secure your safety and your future.

Before you dive in, I want to take a moment to thank you for choosing *Survival 101: Beginner's Guide*. This book is one of many on the market today, and I am grateful and humbled that you have chosen mine. Thank you. Please, enjoy it.

CHAPTER 1

Preparing To Survive

Our present society continues to revolve around broken systems and overdrawn supply chains. While these systems work perfectly when everything is going "as it should," the minute something goes wrong, they rapidly break down. With that being said, the systems have worked, and they have managed to provide us with many excellent tools that we can use to our advantage. Using what is available to you is the first key to surviving. If you live in an urban environment, you have a lot available to you. While it may be challenging for you to access it during the pandemic, much of it is still accessible. It will provide you with a means of safety and survival should anything else go wrong.

Preparing yourself to survive requires you to first educate yourself on what survival will look like for your unique situation. Developing this knowledge will help you recognize the risks and considerations unique to your situation. It will help you maintain a clear action plan for any emergency level you need to address. Remember that survival does not come with a one-size-fits-all solution, so you need to plan for *your* unique circumstances. I will tell you how.

Gauging Your Current Situation

The first order of business when it comes to survival is gauging your current situation so that you know exactly what it is that you need to do to survive. Become aware of what your current lifestyle looks like, where you gather all your supplies, where you store your supplies, and what your exit routes are. What possible risk-factors you face based on your unique circumstances. This way, you know what to be aware of, consider, and manage when addressing emergencies.

If you live in a rural environment, your risk factor could be that you lose contact with the rest of the world so you cannot easily access food, supplies, medical assistance, or any external assistance, should anything go wrong. Alternatively, if you live in an urban environment, your risk factor could be that you do not have enough space to store large amounts of survival tools, your local supply chains for food and supplies could run dry, and your environment could collapse. You could end up hurt, or grid-locked and unable to leave in a timely fashion. Often, the most significant risk to those in rural settings is the risk of being cut off from the rest of the world, which creates a significant threat. At the same time, those in urban environments run the risk of getting too comfortable and not knowing how to protect themselves in case of an emergency. In either scenario, your livelihood could be at serious risk.

As you assess your current situation, pay close attention to how you are accessing the five requirements for survival. Water, shelter, fire, food, and safety need to be your priorities in a survival situation. Fire is considered mandatory for survival as it helps maintain your core temperature. Fire also provides you with a reliable cooking source and a tool that can help people locate you if you find yourself lost and waiting on search and rescue teams.

Once you have defined your current situation, you are going to look for all possible risk factors and then create a plan for how to minimize those risk factors. You need to have a plan for how you are going to secure your five requirements for survival. Having a clear, well-crafted plan ensures that no matter what happens, you feel confident that you can advocate for and take care of your survival. This way, you are never left relying on anyone else and possibly growing ill, injured, or dying as a result.

Measuring Emergency Levels

Measuring emergency levels is vital as it allows you to determine how you execute your response plan. For mild emergencies, the execution of your response will be far less intense than it will be in extreme emergencies. You need to know how to measure and monitor emergencies confidently so that you can take the response that feels right *for you*. Realize that everyone will speculate what they believe the intended threat level is, and that you will likely hear about these speculations all over mass media and throughout society. You need to personally decide what you believe the risk factor is, based on your best-educated guess, and respond accordingly.

Waiting for the authorities to provide you with adequate information regarding your risk level has left many people in dire situations that directly threatened their livelihood. For example, right now, in 2020, it is speculated that if every country had taken the pandemic seriously just two weeks sooner, we would have seen less than half of the impact we see right now. Unfortunately, government and authorities do not always respond to things promptly, so relying on them is not always the right solution. You need to become confident in relying on yourself and your own best judgment to protect yourself in case of an emergency since you alone are responsible for your survival.

In terms of emergencies, there are three levels of emergencies to look out for:

- mild emergencies, which are sometimes called level three emergencies
- moderate emergencies, which are sometimes called level two emergencies
- extreme emergencies, which are sometimes called level one emergencies.

Mild emergencies, also called level three emergencies, are considered isolated, contained critical incidents. These might include something like a single non-life-threatening injury, a fire that was contained or extinguished, or something else that would be considered an emergency, but that is controlled and not actively spreading. At home, this might include a fall, a broken bone, or a flood. In your town, this might include a nearby flood, a single building such as a grocery store or a school catching fire, or something similar. Based on our current emergency with COVID-19, level three of this emergency would have been when the illness was first located in other countries but had not yet spread, and was not yet escalated to a crisis or a pandemic.

Moderate or level two emergencies are considered situational crises. Situational crises are ones that are not developing or worsening. Still, they do require more significant assistance to protect yourself in these circumstances. For example, if a large portion of your home was on fire or there was an uncontained fire in your house, if you had fallen and seriously hurt yourself and were unable to get up to retrieve help, or if you were ill with something like bacterial meningitis. More significant floods and nearby wildfires can also be considered level two emergencies.

A level one emergency or a crisis is a state in which something significant is going on. Hurricanes, major floods, tsunamis, uncontrollable wildfires, and other natural disasters that pose a major threat to peoples' wellbeing are recognized as level one emergencies. Man-made disasters such as active war zones, police states, and pandemics also classify as a level one emergency. In all of these scenarios, you are immediately cut off from all five things you need for survival and are required to manage your own survival until society can come back together *if* society is able to come back together.

Emergencies You Are Most Likely to Come Across

The exact types of emergencies you should be aware of and prepared for depending on where you come from and what your climate and geographical regions are. Each area will have unique natural threats that can rapidly evolve into emergencies and threaten your survival.

If you live in a cold climate or near the arctic circle, you are likely to face emergencies such as wind storms, freezing water, and exposure. Wind storms can be incredibly cold, can blow snow around and create white-outs or blizzards, and can damage things such as trees and create hazards from falling objects. Freezing water can make it impossible for you to source drinking water, or could cause illness or death if you were to fall in and experience hypothermia or frostbite. In some cases, this can happen in mere minutes. Exposure is a danger that can lead to hypothermia and frostbite. Avalanches are another possibility in cold climates, particularly if you live near the mountains. As well, you should consider the fact that food and water supplies may be cut off if you cannot get any imported to you and could be hard to locate due to hunting and foraging becoming far more challenging in the winter.

If you live in the desert, monsoon, drought, haboob, and microbursts can be considered threats to your survival. A monsoon is a heavy rainstorm that typically occurs later in the day and can lead to rapid flooding. This is due to the amount of rain that falls and the fact that the ground is too dry to absorb all of the water adequately. Drought occurs when there is limited or no rainfall for long periods and can lead to dehydration. It can also make growing crops much more challenging. During periods of drought, it can also be hot and dry, which can lead to heatstroke or even death from overheating. Haboobs are giant walls of dust and dirt that can grow as tall as 3,000 feet and stretch miles long, and dust storms often accompany them. The storm itself can put you at risk from exposure by destroying air quality, and they can also damage crops, homes, and other environmental features. Microbursts, on the other hand, are incredibly strong concentrated winds that can tear things down in their path. Microbursts are similar to tornados, but they do not spin in circles as tornados do.

The tropics are well-known for having hurricanes or tropical storms, earthquakes, floods, and windstorms. They can also get monsoon weather, which can increase the risk of flooding and flood-related damages. These natural disasters can be dangerous and routinely cause injuries and fatalities every single year.

Heavily forested areas like what is seen on the west coast of North America and the grassy regions like the prairies or the Midwest are often at the highest risk of dealing with wildfires and earthquakes. Regions that have mountains are at risk of landslides and, during winter seasons, avalanches. Flooding is also frequent in wet forested areas such as those seen along the west coast of North America.

If you live immediately along the coastline, you are at considerable risk of water-related threats. Tsunamis can be a threat, as can hurricanes or earthquakes that lead to flooding. On individual islands, such as those in Hawaii, there is also the risk of a volcano erupting and rendering entire areas of land unlivable for extended periods.

Knowing what types of natural disasters are likely to strike your region allows you to properly prepare for the threats you may face. You should make a plan for how you will face each and every possible disaster in your area, both natural and man-made, so that you have a plan for any unique circumstance you may come up against. Backup plans are also ideal, as they can kick into effect and keep everyone on the same page in case your original plan does not pan out. You find yourself in need of something more significant to protect you.

Preparing for Extreme Emergencies

You and your family need to prepare for extreme emergencies. Being prepared for an extreme emergency ensures that you are ready for mild and moderate emergencies, too, should one occur. Preparing for an emergency requires you to consider four things: your resources, your plan of operations, your escape, and your long term survival. If you can adequately prepare for all four of these aspects of your livelihood, you will have a much stronger chance of surviving any emergency you happen across.

Planning for emergencies requires you to know exactly what resources you need, and how many of those resources you need so that you can accommodate for every person in your household. You need enough food, water, shelter, clothes, medicine, hygiene products, and protection for every single person in your family, as well as anything else you can reasonably bring to aid and simplify survival measures. In long term survival situations, there is no way you will be able to tote in large amounts of food or water for your survival, so you will want to have a plan for how you are going to acquire and sterilize food and water, too. For example, you will want to have hunting supplies and water purifier on hand so that you can safely harvest and consume food and water in a natural environment.

Your plan of operations should be a detailed plan for how you are going to survive in any situation you find yourself in. This includes how you are going to escape if you need to, where you are going to go, and what you are going to do when you get there. Your order of operations is essential as it keeps you organized and focused on doing the most essential things required for your survival in the most important order. You must secure the most critical things first, as everything else can come next. For example, you need to acquire water before food because the average human can survive three weeks without food but only three days without water. Before anything else, though, you need to secure shelter because if your core body temperature drops, you will not be able to secure anything else. Doing everything in proper rule, then, is critical.

In addition to knowing how you are going to survive an emergency, you need to know how you are going to escape one. Many situations will require you to escape to a safer environment until your present environment is safer to return to. Knowing how you will escape is critical, as your survival skills are virtually useless if you are trapped in a dangerous situation. In a rural or coastal setting, your escape might include where you will go and how you will get away should a tornado, hurricane, or another significant storm roll in. In an urban environment, your plan of getaway might consist of how you will get away if you need to leave the urban environment, and everything is at risk of becoming grid-locked. You will also need to consider *when* you will time your escape, as you want to make sure that you go before it is too late. Of course, you do not want to leave too early and find yourself having to rely on survival skills long before you need to, because this can lead to a depletion of your resources.

Finally, you need to prepare for long term survival. If returning to your home is not an option for extended periods of time, you need to feel confident that you can survive until then. Having a plan for how you will support your survival for an extended period ensures that you can survive for as long as you need and that you do not perish in the woods due to a lack of survival knowledge and skills.

The Skills You Will Need

Bushcraft and wilderness skills are vital for your ability to survive an emergency. Knowing how to make a fire, navigate the wilderness, trap, track, build shelter, and use wilderness tools will help you accomplish everything you need to survive. I discuss all of these skills in far greater detail in my book *Survival 101: Bushcraft*. Gardening is another great skill to have, as well as knowing how to preserve food for extended periods of time. I discuss these topics in my books *Survival 101: Raised Bed Gardening 2020* and *Survival 101: Food Storage*. Foraging and scavenging for food in a natural environment is also a great skill to have as it ensures that you are able to select a variety of food sources and that you do not have to rely solely on animal proteins or wait excessive periods of time for your food to start growing.

The key to surviving in the wilderness and living off the land is realizing that there will be multiple skills that are relevant to your survival. Not only are you going to need to know about *what* has to be done, but you are also going to need to know-*how*. This means that by learning how to build a shelter, for example, you also need to know how to use an ax and a saw properly, how to properly secure things in place, and how to use other resources such as rope and knot tying to create a safe environment. The more skills you know, the more likely you will be to survive in the wilderness for as long as you need to. We will discuss all of these skills, and more, between *Chapter 3: The First Five*, and *Chapter 5: The 34 Tasks of Survival*.

CHAPTER 2

Key Terms

As you read through the remainder of this book, you are going to come across many terms that may seem unusual or foreign to you. These terms are commonly used in survival situations to define certain circumstances, tasks, or objects that are relevant to a survival scenario. Before we dig any deeper into survival itself, we are going to discuss what these key terms are and why they are pertinent to your survival.

Area of Operation (AO)

Area of Operation (AO) defines the area where your operations take place. This term was first described by the U.S. armed forces parlance to establish an operational area where the armed forces would be conducting their operational tasks. In an emergency, your AO refers to the area you are leaving, the area you are going to, and the area you will be passing through to get there. Your AO will define the entire area in which you will be surviving. This includes where you will sleep, cook, fetch water, hunt, and otherwise live for the duration of the emergency.

You should have a clearly defined AO, and no one should leave the AO at any given time without a clear procedure and reason as to why they are leaving. Leaving without a proper plan could result in someone getting lost or becoming exposed to unexpected threats due to being in an area that you are not used to or comfortable in. There should also be a clearly defined set of trails and roads within the AO that will determine where you go at all times, and everyone should stay on those trails and paths. Leaving them could result in becoming lost or injured as well.

A-Team

Your A-Team, when it comes to survival, relates to every single person who will be coming with you in a survival setting, and it refers to the hierarchy or operational order inside of that team. While you might think the only people you will care about in a survivalist setting will be those in your immediate household, it is ideal to have at least one or two other families who will be joining you. You should all have a clear plan for how you will survive once you reach the wilderness, and what each of you is going to do to aid survival. There is strength in numbers, even in the wilderness, so having additional members of your A-Team should always be welcomed and supported.

Having a clearly defined hierarchy in your A-Team ensures that everyone knows who to listen to and what their role is for the survival of the team. The last thing you need is to come up against dominance struggles or miscommunications in the wilderness, so you want to have this sorted out beforehand. Everyone should do what they know best, which means the leaders of your group should include people who are knowledgeable about survival and who are capable of giving orders and guiding the team in a practical but compassionate manner. Aside from that, you should have people committed to cooking, hunting, foraging, fetching water, gardening, building, and performing other survival-related tasks. While one person can certainly take on multiple tasks, it is essential to avoid giving one person more functions than anyone else. This can lead to that person burning out and everyone suffering as a result. Everyone should take on an equal task load and do their part to contribute to the survival of everyone at the camp.

Bug Out Hideout Site (BOHS)

A Bug Out Hideout Site (BOHS) is essential for you to survive an emergency. The military first described the BOHS in the 1950s. Now, it is used by the preparedness community as a way to define the location that a family will escape to should anything go wrong.

Ideally, your BOHS should be identified in advance and should be well-known by those who will be surviving with you, and *only* by those who will be surviving with you. If possible, a well-developed BOHS will already have shelter in place, and everyone who will be surviving there should know how to get there safely and navigate the area around it.

You should define your BOHS in advance and get comfortable in the area, as this will increase your confidence in surviving in this space. When everyone is clear and familiar with the area, it is easier to execute survival tasks because everyone is already familiar with where everything is. Therefore, it is quicker to get yourselves set up and cover your essentials faster. The looming pressure of an emergency can make traveling and surviving more challenging, so having this confidence in your BOHS location means you do not have to rely on your logic during an emergency because it all comes back through memory.

Emergency Rallying Point (ERP)

An emergency rallying point (ERP) is where you are going to rally in the case of an emergency. You will define your ERP based on what emergencies you are likely to face in your environment and where the safest rallying point would be. You should have an ERP for your household, and an ERP for anyone who would be going to your BOHS with you, including any members of your A-Team. This way, the members of your household can gather quickly in mild to moderate emergencies. The members of your family and other A-Team members can gather quickly in moderate to extreme emergencies where evacuation is required. Your ERP will be far closer than your BOHS, and you and your A-Team will travel from the ERP to the BOHS together to ensure safety and security.

Grab and Go Bag (GnG Bag)

A Grab and Go Bag (GnG Bag) is essential for an emergency where you do not have enough time to pack up all of your gear and head to your ERP or your BOHS. In some emergencies, such as natural disasters, there is no time for you to gather everything and head to your ERP, so you must grab your GnG Bag and go.

Your GnG Bag should have the absolute essentials for your survival, including things like:

- Ready to eat non-perishable food
- Drinking water
- Solar-powered phone charger
- Crank radio
- Crank flashlight
- Extra batteries
- Personal toiletries
- Personal medications
- First-aid kit
- Copy of the emergency plan
- Documents including insurance papers and personal identification
- Garbage bags
- Moist towelettes
- Cash in small bills
- Seasonal clothing

- Emergency blanket
- Sturdy footwear
- Dust mask
- Whistle
- Flare.

You should also have a "help/OK" sign to display in your window so that if you are trapped in your home during an emergency situation, you can display this in your window for safety. This way, if emergency crews come by and see "help," they know that you or someone inside of your dwelling is in need of immediate help, and they can prioritize helping you.

Immediate Rallying Point (IRP)

An immediate rallying point (IRP) differs from the ERP because it will be closer to home. An ERP should be removed enough from your immediate vicinity that if an emergency strikes, you can remove yourself from that emergency space before it harms you. For example, if you have a few hours or days of warning before a wildfire comes through your town, you can use your ERP. In some scenarios, the crisis may not be large enough to warrant leaving your immediate vicinity, or it may be so large that it is now too dangerous to leave. For these scenarios, you need an IRP which will be in your immediate vicinity. An underground storm shelter beneath your house would be a great example of an IRP.

You should have two IRP's defined: one for scenarios where you can stay in your own home and one for situations where you must leave it. Have a clearly defined IRP so that everyone in your home knows where to find everyone else. This is especially important if you have a large household, as certain disasters can shred homes and leave various rooms a threat. You would not want to lose someone in a different room of your house because you did not know they were there. If you cannot stay in your home, your locale will have storm shelters or emergency shelters where you can go for safekeeping. Determine which shelter you and your family will use in case of an emergency so that if any of you are not home when the emergency strikes, you can feel confident that you will all find your way back together. Hopefully, you will be able to leave the IRP for the ERP and the BOHS after things settle down.

CHAPTER 3

The First Five

As soon as you find yourself in a survival situation, you must immediately focus on fulfilling the five things that are most important to your survival. These five things include water, shelter, fire, food, and safety. Without either of these five things, you face the risk of becoming severely ill or even dying as they are all crucial to your survival. It is essential to understand that how you access and secure such things in an urban environment will differ from a natural environment. Knowing how to obtain these five things for yourself and your A-Team will ensure that you remain safe and that you can protect yourself under any circumstance.

The First Five Urban VS. Off-Grid Environments

Naturally, how you secure water, shelter, fire, food, and safety is going to differ between urban and natural or off-grid environments. In an urban environment, some of what you need is supplied by the city you live in and will already be standing. In contrast, in a natural environment, you will be solely responsible for accessing everything you need.

In an urban situation, you are going to need to account for the fact that you have limited space. However, you will have access to shelter that is already built and secured, which makes it easier for you to secure a place to stay. You will need to check the quality of your shelter to ensure it is safe, though, and protected from external dangers. If you are not, you will need to make immediate repairs or adjustments to secure your safety and survival.

Aside from the shelter, most urban environments have built-in supply chains for water, food, electricity, and safety. When you come across a survival emergency, all four of these things can disappear, and, in some cases, the shelter can, too. For example, during a hurricane, you might find your accommodation damaged, which means you need to find somewhere else to stay.

When your supply chains for water, food, electricity, and safety are destroyed, you have to discover a new means of securing water, food, fire, and protection. If you are lucky, you may already have a stocked pantry with purified water that you stored in case of an emergency. However, you are still going to need to source as much of these things as you possibly can. In a long term emergency, this may include sending two people out to a nearby rural environment to fish or trap animal proteins and forage for plant proteins. Water can also be challenging to source in an urban environment, particularly if your water lines have been damaged, shut off, or contaminated. Ideally, you should be able to access water from a nearby river or stream. However, you should assume that it is contaminated from urban runoff sources, so you will need to purify it properly. In a situation where your electricity is off, you will need to use fire for cooking and heat. During these types of emergencies, take note of whether or not you have any natural gas supplied to your house. If you do, check to make sure there are no gas leaks, as gas leaks lead to fatalities. As well, make sure there are no active powerlines or livewires, which could lead to a dangerous or fatal electric shock. Finally, you need to consider your safety in an urban environment when it comes to external forces. If you find yourself in a police state, you need to consider your safety against the authorities. If you find yourself in a long term survival situation, you need to be cautious of looters who will rob people of their resources in a means to secure their survival.

If you are not in an urban environment when a survival emergency strikes, or if you have left your urban environment, you are going to have to be single-handedly responsible for everything associated with your survival. You need to build shelter, secure water, build a fire, harvest food, and protect yourself from any threats in the environment. Ultimately, you will be starting from scratch using any tools and resources you were able to bring and all of the resources available to you in the wilderness. Fortunately, since we are mammals, everything you need to survive is underfoot. Hence, even if you have to escape with nothing but the clothes off your back, there is still hope for survival.

Shelter

The shelter is the first thing you need to secure, as daytime rapidly turns into nighttime, and nighttime is when you are at your most significant risk. In any environment, the night is when temperatures drop. If you are already enduring cold weather, these drops can be deadly.

In an urban environment, nighttime is when people are asleep. Therefore, they are least prepared for anything that might happen. If a natural disaster strikes, you will be less alert and prepared, as will everyone around you. In terms of human dangers, the night is when people are more likely to ambush you or attempt to rob you, making it a more significant threat. In a natural environment, nighttime temperatures get even cooler since your heat will not be entirely as secure as an urban shelter would be. Animals who tend to hunt at night will have an advantage on you by having better eyesight, sharper senses, and a more exceptional ability to attack and defend themselves during the evening. Having a safe place to stay is crucial to protect you against any nighttime threats.

If you are surviving in an urban setting, there are four types of shelter you can use. Ideally, you should remain in your home as your primary shelter, which should be your absolute goal. The only time you should leave your home is if it becomes damaged or has to for some dire reason. Otherwise, this is where you should remain. The second possible shelter, if you have to leave your home, would be to stay with a family member or a friend in their home. This way, you know who you are staying with, and feel comfortable supporting each other and surviving together. If a family member or friend is not possible, you may be able to stay with a neighbor who has room for you. However, you should beware of the fact that trying to stay with a neighbor could be hit or miss. The third option would be to stay in a local shelter. When natural disasters strike, municipal governments will set up local shelters for people to remain in if their own homes are uninhabitable, and you can stay there. Note that these environments will offer minimal means for independence, and you will have to abide by the rules, which may or may not contradict what you believe to be right for your survival. The fourth option for shelter would be to find an empty home that no one lives in and take it over as your own for the duration of your survival emergency. However, this should be an absolute last resort as it can lead to legal issues and other dangers, such as the homeowner removing you by force. Finally, if you cannot secure a sanctuary where you are, you should retreat to a natural environment and secure shelter there.

In the wilderness, securing shelter requires some consideration. Namely, you need to pick a spot that factors in the five W's which are necessary for survival in any wilderness situation. The five W's are wood, water, weather, widowmakers, and wildlife.

The best location to build your shelter is one with plenty of wood available. Wood is an excellent building material and fuel for fires. Plus, building your shelter in a forest means the trees will protect you from most weather fronts.

Water is essential for your survival, so you need to set up camp somewhere where you can easily access water, as you do not want to be dragging gallons of water along a lengthy, steep path back to shelter. However, make sure the water is downhill from where you are so you are not at risk of floods or sleeping on continually moist grounds.

You must take the weather seriously, as the weather is the number one cause for people dying in the wilderness. Death by exposure is severe, painful, and happens rapidly. Consider the climate of the area you are in and plan your shelter accordingly. You need to be safely shaded away from the hot sun, protected from rainfall, and kept warm and insulated in a cold or snowy environment. Build accordingly and build quickly. The most accessible shelter to build for wet weather is a lean-to, though A-frame tents work well. To construct a lean-to, you will simply hang a tarp from four trees, with one side of the tarp being higher than the other. If your tarp is long enough, or if you have an extra tarp, you can run the lower end of the tarp to the ground to give you a comfortable, dry spot at the back of the lean-to. Build an A-Frame tent by finding five Y-shaped logs and one straight log. You want to prop your five Y-shaped logs up by having the first, third, and fifth logs with the Y-shape down so that they have one single branch end up in the air. The second and fourth logs should be upside down with two arms in the air and strapped to the first and fifth log. This way, you can stabilize your structure. Lay the single, long log in the crook of the Y-shaped logs, so it runs across the top of the shelter like a roof beam. You can then cover the entire shelter with a tarp if you have one. If not, you can use spruce needle branches with the needles still on, leafy branches, twigs, moss, and long grasses to help build a roof over your shelter. In particularly wet or cold situations, you should combine a tarp with a naturally-built roof to provide insulation and protect you from the damp weather. If you are in a cold condition, digging a small cave into a snowbank is the best option for shelter. Refrain from digging it out to be too deep, as this can cause the snow to collapse and can trap you inside, causing certain death.

Widowmakers are natural threats in the wilderness that can instantly injure or kill you. For example, if you build a snow hut that is too deep and the snow collapses, you have died as the result of a widowmaker. Trees and branches that are starting to fall over can fall at random or with a small wind gust, and they can also injure or kill anyone in their path. Rockslides, mudslides, and avalanches can also be widowmakers, so you will want to assess your risk for these threats and protect yourself if need be. Never set up camp in a spot where any of these threats are looming, as they can lead to accidental injury or death.

Finally, you need to consider wildlife when you are in the wilderness. Avoid building your camp in a space where wildlife frequents. "Wildlife highways" as they are called stomped-out paths and clearings in the wilderness, where a variety of wildlife frequents. Camping too close to one could result in untimely or unwanted meetings between you and wild animals, which could pose a severe threat to your safety. Camping nearby to these wildlife highways is a good idea as it puts you relatively close to a spot where you can easily trap wildlife for food, but do not get too close. It is a good idea to educate yourself on local wildlife, so you know what to expect and how to protect yourself properly. So you know what type of wildlife is available to harvest and eat if you find yourself in a survival emergency.

Water

After you secure shelter, water is the next most crucial thing. The only time water comes before accommodation is if you will be escaping an urban environment to survive, in which case both water and food should come first if you are capable of securing purified water and non-perishable, ready-to-eat food items. Otherwise, locating a source of water becomes your next order of operation.

In an urban environment, you can generally source water directly from the tap, even during emergency situations. Even so, you should keep an ample amount of bottled or canned water on hand so that if you ever find yourself unable to access water, you can safely consume the water you have stored. More often than not, government and rescue organizations will come through with a safe quantity of drinking water within hours or days of an emergency striking.

With that being said, they will have limited supply. They may not be able to find you, or you may not be able to find them, so you need to be prepared to source your water if and when your water supply runs out. If you cannot access water from your tap, look for a nearby stream, creek, or river. Lakes, ponds, or man-made waterbodies will work. Still, the water is more likely to be contaminated, so be sure to properly purify it first.

It is essential that no matter where you harvest water from in an urban environment that you assume that water is highly contaminated. Urban environments have a variety of chemical runoffs that contaminate all water sources, including the rain. Tap water is treated for these runoffs, but in an emergency, situation treatment can become faulty or ineffective. For that reason, you need to treat *all* water if you are facing a moderate to extreme emergency. Having testing strips handy at home is essential in an urban environment as it will allow you to check your water for chemicals. You should test tap water to monitor that it continues to be safe to use, and stop using it or start treating it the minute it becomes unsafe. If you are going to need to survive for an extended period of time, and have access to multiple water sources, test each source to see which will be the cleanest. You will still need to purify it, but this will ensure that you are least likely to drink contaminated water and wind up sick.

In a natural environment, water needs to be sourced from a natural water source. Springwater from creeks, streams, rivers, and waterfalls are ideal as the movement of the water prevents bacteria and parasites from building up in them. Water such as lakes, ponds, and large pools are often the least safe, as they can become contaminated, and there is no way for the contaminants to move out. However, if that is all you have access to, then it will have to do.

Always assume that all water in a natural setting is contaminated and treat it to avoid getting sick. Even if you are drinking from a crystal clear stream, creek, river, or waterfall, you never know if a dead animal or other contaminant is upstream, and that can get into your water.

Getting sick in a survival situation is a sure way to put your survival at-risk, so you want to avoid it as much as possible. Always treat *all* water, but be particularly careful in treating water sourced from still bodies of water. You should treat water with proper filters designed for hikers; however, you can boil the water for 20 minutes over a fire if you do not have access to filters.

Fire

Fire is essential for survival because it provides two benefits: heat and a cooking source. You can also use the fire to sterilize things either through the smoke or through boiling water to clean off equipment such as stainless steel cookware. If you are in an urban setting and continue to have access to power, you will replace fire with electricity. If not, however, you will switch it out for fire.

In an urban environment, you may have the capacity to have a fire in your own home if you have a fireplace. Keep wood nearby and have plenty of starting materials and combustion tools on hand so you can start and maintain fire as needed. Lint out of your dryer is excellent for an urban starting material, as is cotton, cardboard tubes, and tissue papers. If you have a gas fireplace, check for leakages in the fuel line before using it, as some emergencies can damage the leak, and the gas from your fireplace is deadly. As well, gas fireplaces will not work as a cooking source, so you will need access to something else to cook your food with.

If you do not have a fireplace in your house, your next order of business is to look for a grill. Barbecues will provide a source of heat when outdoors, as well as a means for cooking. If you do not have access to a barbecue, you should build a firepit safely away from your building, but close enough that you can use it for heat and cooking. For the inside of your house, candles work as a light source and provide a small source of heat if you have enough candles or large enough candles. For warmth, bundle up on extra bedding and clothes if it happens to be a cold night. Standing out next to your fire with thick clothes and a blanket can help heat them, so you are likely to stay warm throughout the entire night. You can also sleep skin-to-skin alongside other humans if it is unusually cold to protect your core temperature and help keep you alive.

In a natural environment, a fire will provide a means of heat, an opportunity for you to keep yourself clean, and a spot for you to cook. Your heating fire should be kept near your camp. In contrast, your cooking fire and food should be at least 100 yards away from where you are sleeping to avoid attracting wildlife directly to your sleeping quarters. This way, if wildlife comes across your food, and they will, they do not come across you at the same time.

Creating a fire in the woods requires a certain amount of skill as you have to know how to build a fire so it will start, how to light your fire, and how to maintain it without accidentally smothering it. To thrive, fires rely on what is called the triangle of fire, which means they need oxygen, fuel, and heat. With these three elements, your fire will thrive, and without them, it will either go out or fail to get started in the first place.

There are two fire lays you can use that will help you get started, though I go over three additional ones in *Survival 101: Bushcraft*. These two fire lays are called the teepee fire, and the log cabin fire. A teepee fire is best for heat, while a log cabin fire is best for cooking.

Before you can light a fire, you are going to need what is known as a tinder bird nest, which is a starter for any fire. A tinder bird nest uses starting materials such as dry grass, twigs, cotton, dried pine cones, dried tree bark, and the lichen known as old man's beard. You want to take all of these materials and form a small birds nest shape using them, as this will give you plenty of starting materials to get your fire going. The idea with any fire is to get the tinder burning first, then the kindling, and then the actual fuel logs. From there, you can continue to add logs to your already burning fire to keep it going.

The teepee fire lay is created by taking a bird's nest and placing it in the center of where you want your fire to be. Then, use kindling to form a teepee shape over the tinder. You will continue doing this until you have used pencil-sized twigs. Then you will create a more massive teepee around your kindling structure using actual logs, which will be the fuel for your fire. After you have created this structure, you can light the tinder on the innermost part of your teepee, and that fire will reach up to burn your kindling, then your fuel logs. From there, you will have a roaring fire.

A log cabin style fire lay is created by interlocking logs to create a cabin style fire lay. To create your log cabin fire lay, you are going to use smaller pieces of wood, not much larger than tinder. You will lay two pieces of wood parallel to each other on the ground and far enough apart to create a space between them but close enough that when you lay more kindling across them, the second layer of kindling comfortably rests with either end on the previous kindling. Your second layer of kindling should be laid out as two pieces of kindling crossing over the ends of the first layer, creating a square shape. Continue layering kindling in either direction until you have about 5-8 layers. You want enough there to start a reasonable fire, but not so much that it takes a while to burn. The goal with a log cabin fire lay is that it burns down quickly so that you can cook on a low fire and the embers at the base of the fire. You can start your log cabin fire lay by placing a tinder bird nest in the center and lighting the fire, which will then catch the wood on fire. Make sure your bird nest is large enough to reach the fire you have laid around it. You can always tighten the inner square by placing the logs closer together if need be.

Food

If you have enough time left on your day of arrival, you will want to go in search of food right away. Ideally, you should have at least a couple of hours left before nightfall to avoid being caught away from camp in the dark. If you do not have someone who can stay at the camp and monitor the fire while you go in search of food, you are going to want to wait on building your fire until you return. If you do not have enough time before nightfall, you will make your fire right away, sleep through the night, then start on finding food first thing in the morning.

In an urban environment, you want to account for your food by having at least two weeks' worth of food in your pantry at all times. Once you have two weeks' worth of food stored, you want to move on to storing enough food for a few months or up to a year. It may sound like a lot, but the reality is that you never know how much you will need. Having more than enough is always better than having none at all.

If you are in an urban environment and an emergency strikes and you have not yet stored everything you need, you are going to need to find a way to source food. The first and possibly most obvious means of searching is to look in local grocery stores and markets for food. If the stores have not shut down, prioritize buying sale items of non-perishable ready to eat foods. This way, you can buy enough for the foreseeable future. If the emergency you are facing has shut down or diminished grocery stores, you can look to nearby towns for farmers who may have what you need. In many emergencies, charitable organizations will rapidly come through and offer food and water to those who have been affected. However, there is always a chance that this does not work out for you. For example, if you are not located or if they run out of resources, you will need to rely on yourself for your food and water. If it comes to it, you can look to hunt and forage your foods using the same means that natural survivalists will need to do. Be extremely cautious when foraging or trapping food in urban environments to avoid breaking laws or accidentally injuring someone else, or becoming injured in the process. Avoid using dangerous weapons in favor of trapping, fishing, and foraging, which are all much safer means of gathering food in an urban environment. They do not pose a threat to other humans in the area.

Sourcing food in a natural environment is a large undertaking. Learning to forage, fish, and trap is the best way to get started. Foraging is perhaps the easiest undertaking when it comes to acquiring food, as you only need to source the food, you do not need to do much to prepare it. In the wilderness, there are hundreds of plants that are healthy for you to eat, and there are hundreds more that are dangerous for you to eat. The only safe way to know what is available for you is to find a book on local foraging or take a local foraging class to discover what to look for, how to harvest the foraging items, and how to consume them safely. Many times, you can find herbalists who offer plant walks that will educate you on how to safely forage food in your local area. They can answer any questions you may have when it comes to safely sourcing food in the wilderness.

Fishing and trapping are slightly more challenging as you have to prepare the food you find, both through gutting it and through cooking it properly to avoid becoming sick. It is advised that upon leaving an urban environment, you bring fishing line and hooks with you, as well as snare wires for trapping. With your fishing lines and hooks, you will want to tie the line along the end of a sturdy stick and make it long enough that you can dangle it out in the water. Then, you will tie your hook on the other end and attach a piece of bait to it. A small bug like a worm or a caterpillar will work perfectly. Look for an area of water where it is relatively still, such as an inlet on a river or a deeper, slower-moving part of a creek. Then, dangle your line! You might need to bob it in and out a few times to encourage fish to bite, but soon enough, someone will bite. If not, see if you can find a similar area that may be more densely populated.

To prepare a fish for eating, you will rub the back of your knife along the flesh of the fish to remove the scales. Then, you will start at the tail end of the fish by inserting your knife in to make an incision. Make your incision deep enough that it goes into the middle of the fish, but not so deep that you completely cut the fish in half. Remove the innards and gills from the fish with your hand, then chop off the head and tail. Rinse it off and cook it thoroughly so that it is safe for eating.

Snares are set by tying a noose into snare wire and placing a snare somewhere that small to medium game animals are likely to frequent. Then, you mostly wait for one to trap itself and die in the snare. The most popular game to attract in snares are rabbits and hares, though you might also use snares to capture squirrels, rats, or other rodents.

Creating your snare noose will require you first to create the noose itself. Snare wire will work best for this, but twisted copper from inside small appliance power cords, picture hanging wire, craft wire, and headphone wire work, too. You will start your snare by creating a loop on one end of the wire. With wire, you will make a loop at twist the wire several times over to make sure the loop is strong enough, as you do not want it to break when the animal begins to struggle. Otherwise, you will lose the animal. Next, you are going to thread the other end of the wire through the loop you have made. The loop should be able to freely move up and down the wire, as this is how it will tighten when an animal begins to run or struggle inside of the snare.

You want to set your snare with the leader line, or the end of the snare that is not actively contributing to the noose loop, tied tightly to a branch or a part of brush that will not break under the pressure of the snare being activated by the animal. Then, the noose itself should be set open, ideally hooked around a small twig or something near the ground to keep the snare open and in place. When an animal runs through the snare, it will tighten, effectively trapping the animal.

Once you have trapped a small animal, you need to process it. You will need rope to hang the animal, heavy-duty scissors and two knives: a smaller one for precision cutting, and a larger one for cutting through joints. You will need a container for the rabbit parts you will keep and one for the parts you won't want. The container for the parts you will keep should have cold, filtered water in it. The other one should be easy enough to transport the discarded animal parts far away from your camp to avoid attracting any wild animals in your direction.

You will start by hanging the animal with rope by their back legs over a low hanging branch, which will make it easy for you to access the animal and process it. For a rabbit, you will cut the head and two front feet off so it can bleed out through the feet. For anything else, you can sever the arteries and veins in their throat. Once the bleeding stops, you will cut around the back legs down to the meat layer using a small precision knife. Then, you will pull the hide off of the animal. You may need to use the knife to carefully cut the pelt away from the skin at some points, but gently tugging it off should work for the most part. You will also cut from the inner thigh across to the bellybutton so that as you pull the pelt off the genital area remains covered in hair. Go to the back of the rabbit and do the same thing, leaving fur around the anus and tail area. At this point, the pelt should easily slide off since the front feet and head are not in place to stop the hide from moving. With rabbits and hares, you can cut the pelt so that it hangs flat and dry it out to be used for future projects if you will be surviving long term. These pelts are excellent for warming up the insides of shelters, sewing together to create warm clothing, and using for other similar purposes.

If you are cooking a small animal like a squirrel, you will not remove the limbs. You will only gut the animal. If you are preparing a larger animal like a rabbit or a hare, you will start by removing the front legs from the animal and placing them in your meat bucket. Use your larger, sturdier knife to sever the ligaments and pry the leg from the body. Next, take your knife and run it down the backbone from the tail to the clavicle bone. You want the cut about as deep as the animal's ribs; then, you will cut this back strip out by tracing the shape just under the ribs. This will give you two pieces of back meat.

Next, you will turn the animal around and start to harvest the organs. Since the lower portions of the animal are removed already, this part is more straightforward. A ruptured organ will require you to discard any meat contaminated by the fluids from that ruptured organ, so you need to be careful. At least this way, you have about four useful pieces of meat already off the animal if you make a mistake. You will start by cutting a small hole into the stomach lining, taking care to only go through the skin layer. Then, you will insert a finger into the hole press the inner organs away from the stomach lining so that you can carefully cut the lining open. You will then use your hands to pull the organs out of the meat. While you can eat the heart and liver, you do not have to. You can discard these if you prefer not to. Simply tug the organs out and away from the animal with a firm tug, and they should all come out safely without rupturing. Throw them away. Finally, remove the hind legs of the animal, then toss the tail and lower spinal portion into your discard bin. Now you are done!

You will want to properly wash your harvested meat, and safely discard the rest of it far away from your camp. Properly wash everything that you used to harvest the animal, too, to avoid any animals tracking you by the scent of the animal you harvested.

You should always cook game meat and fish well beyond what you would cook at home, as it has been wildly harvested, and may have bacteria or parasites growing in it. For game meat, always char the outsides and cook it until the insides are nearly dry. This way, you properly kill any bacteria or parasites that may be lingering in the meat, and that has the potential to make you sick.

Store your meat in proper containers at least 100 yards away from camp. The safest way to do so is to wrap them up in a tarp and hang them out from a branch where they will be too high to be grabbed from the ground and too low to be seized from the branch. This way, no animals can steal your harvested food. Make sure the meat is stored properly in ample amounts of salt, as this prevents it from developing bacteria while you store it. If you cannot adequately store your food, only harvest what you can eat in a few hours on a day to day basis.

Safety

Securing your safety in a survival setting is of utmost importance. Exposure, wildlife, natural disasters, illness, injury, and possible ambush from other humans are all things to consider in various survival circumstances. You can protect yourself by maintaining proper hygiene, and by being prepared to defend yourself in case of an attack. Otherwise, you can protect yourself by steering clear of areas where natural disasters are likely to occur and having a proper shelter in place for you to protect yourself from exposure.

In an urban setting, protecting yourself is reasonably easy because you have access to an abundance of homes to protect you from such things. The main things you will need to look for are leaks, contamination, bacteria, and attacks from the outside world. Gas leaks, pipe leaks, down powerlines feeding live electricity into the ground, and contaminated water, are all common risks when a natural disaster has struck. You need to immediately look for and be aware of any of these things happening so you can protect yourself adequately. Bacteria can come into the house or can grow in the house from inadequate practices such as improper food storage or removal of refuse. Maintaining proper hygiene is imperative to avoid having bacteria build-up and creating a hazard in your life.

If you are in a situation where other humans could harm you, you need to be prepared to protect yourself. Weaponry such as guns, knives, and bows should be considered. Bars on your windows and proper locks on your doors can also protect you from people trying to break in.

In a natural environment, you need to protect yourself from exposure, wildlife, widowmakers, and illness or injury. You can do this with adequate shelter, fire, and proper clothes to keep yourself warm and dry. Having defensive weaponry on hand is essential in case an animal comes through your camp. Protecting yourself by keeping all food sources and scents far away from camp is important, too. You should always change out of the clothes you have cooked and eaten in and leave them at your cooking camp 100 yards away, so you do not accidentally bring the smell back to your sleeping camp with you. Staying away from common areas where animals hang out is ideal, too, as it keeps you protected from the animals who may be passing by. With widowmakers, you already know to avoid them when you are setting up camp. However, you should also be prepared to avoid them when you are traveling, especially if there is wind, rain, or snow. These can encourage dead trees to fall and can injure or kill you while you are away from camp. Prevent injuries by wearing proper footwear, walking on firm ground, moving intentionally and slowly, and protecting your skin from cuts and scrapes. Even one tiny scratch can become infected and lead to death in the wilderness, so avoid them at all costs.

In addition to preventing injury, you also need to prevent illness by maintaining proper core temperature, keeping yourself warm and dry. Promptly care for any wounds you sustain by keeping them clean and dry. You should also properly cleanse any food and water you are going to eat or drink, hang your bedding and clothes in the sun for the sun to sterilize them, and bathe yourself in campfire smoke, which can sterilize any bacteria that may be on your body. These are all essential ways of keeping up hygiene so you do not end up sick, which can quickly become a deadly situation in the wilderness.

CHAPTER 4
The Task Lists

Survival situations are not straightforward or simple. There are many tasks to secure your survival. There are 34 tasks to do if you are going to survive any situation you happen upon. Some of these tasks will need to be completed in advance, while others will need to be completed or finished in the event of an emergency. You will want to run through it in full, first, to prepare yourself, then run through it again in a survival setting to ensure that everything has been adequately completed. In this chapter, we will address the order and importance of each of these 34 tasks. In *Chapter 5: The 34 Tasks of Survival*, we will cover exactly how to fulfill each of these tasks.

Tasks 1 to 3: Preparing

The first three tasks on the task list are all about preparation. These two tasks can and should be done well in advance of anything going wrong, and should be stored in an area where they are easily accessible for mild, moderate, and extreme emergencies.

Although preparing may seem like a small, unimportant task, it is essential to understand that preparation is imperative to your success in a survival situation. During a period where no threats are looming, preparing for survival is easy. At this point, you can access everything you would need in an emergency, place it together in an easily-accessible location, and ensure it is ready for a possible emergency to strike.

People often make the mistake of pretending they have all the time in the world to prepare, which results in procrastination and a failure to ever truly prepare. As a result, when an emergency strikes, they find themselves lacking everything they need. During those scary moments when time is of the essence, they either do not have the time to access essential emergency preparedness items, or the supplies have sold out, such as with the pandemic of 2020. Waiting is often a dangerous game that can lead to an emergency becoming worse than it needs to be, or possibly leading to fatalities because essential preparedness items were not available.

The moral of the story is, do not wait until an emergency to prepare yourself. Assume that an emergency is coming at the least expected of moments, because they can and will, and prepare yourself accordingly. Ensure you are always prepared so that if you ever need your preparedness items, you are ready to go. It is better to be overprepared rather than underprepared in a true emergency.

Tasks 4 to 5: Assessing

Tasks four and five require you to assess the area of the emergency, and each person involved in your survival team. In mild emergencies, a quick area check involves checking the status of everyone involved in the emergency. In extreme settings, this could include checking everyone's abilities and needs, as well as their overall physical condition so that you know who can do what, and what needs have to be considered for survival. Environmentally, you want to check the area to ensure that you know where your essentials can be found.

During an emergency, it may seem impossible or unreasonable to assess the situation. Your emotions may have you wanting to dive right in and immediately get to work, especially if the emergency is dire and time is of the essence. Failure to assess an emergency before jumping into the situation can lead to a far greater emergency than you initially started with. For example, if someone has fallen down a cliff and is sitting at the bottom, injured, attempting to scale the cliff yourself could lead to you also being injured. Neither of you being able to call for help. Although your instinct may tell you to immediately rescue that person, the better idea is to ensure you have adequate help and resources to help that person safely. This way, you do not end up with a larger and more damaging emergency.

Assessment in an emergency survival situation should include assessing yourself and the individuals you are partaking in the survival situation with. Especially if you will be required to survive in the woods for any period of time, you need to know what everyone is capable of and what everyone's limits are. Failure to adequately assess capabilities and limits could lead to a lack of resources being acquired due to someone being incapable, or someone finding themselves facing a medical emergency due to pushing their limits too hard. Although survival situations are trying and limits will inevitably be pushed, you should avoid pushing them too far as this can lead to tragic circumstances and unnecessary illness, injury, or even death.

Tasks 6 to 12: Prevention

Prevention and prevention checklists are used to ensure that everything is kept safe when you are in a survival setting. This includes preventing firearm injuries, fires, drowning, and poisoning. You also need to assess the environment to be aware of and prevent damage from environmental threats, and those that could be caused by man-made threats. In addition to environmental threats, you need to prevent anyone from being injured or falling ill due to improper practices.

Understand that adequate prevention will come in the form of practical measures taken to avoid illness or injury, as well as adequate education on situations that could lead to potential illness or injury. For example, with firearms, sufficient measures such as using the safety or keeping inactive firearms in a locked safe are essential as a practical means of preventing accidental injury or death. Likewise, adequate education on behalf of anyone who might be using the firearm can prevent accidental injury or death caused by improper usage of a dangerous weapon.

As with preparation, ensure that these measures are met ahead of time. Any prevention measures that involve an educational aspect to ensure total prevention is achieved should be learned before a survival situation arises. This ensures that in the heat of a stressful and often scary situation, you are not pressured to attempt to learn new information. During times of high stress, the human mind is not typically capable of absorbing new information, which means that there is a higher risk of mistakes occurring, and therefore illness, injury, or even death could occur.

Should you plan on surviving with other people outside of your household, ensure that they also take prevention seriously. In some cases, such as with foodborne illnesses or improper firearm use, another person's improper education and prevention could lead to yours or someone else's accidentally illness, injury, or death. Ensuring that everyone is properly educated and capable of following essential security measures is the only way to guarantee near-perfect prevention measures are applied in a dangerous situation.

Tasks 13 to 14: Communication

Communication must be secured between the A-Team and, if possible, the outside world. This can be done by securing an emergency radio and ensuring someone is available to listen to it at all times. It can also be done by creating a code word list which will be used by the A-Team to identify certain situations. This, in a sense, is used as your own language so that the A-Team can communicate quickly and promptly.

An essential step in securing communication involves understanding the psychology of an individual during an emergency situation. Recognize that high stress can reduce the quality of communication, creating a higher instance for arguments, as well as miscommunications that could lead to dangerous situations. Accommodate for this by frequently discussing communication measures that will be taken in an emergency situation to minimize miscommunications and avoid arguments.

It may also be beneficial to discuss how each member of the A-Team navigates stress. Understanding each other's tendencies during stressful situations ensures that instinctive stress responses in each individual are not taken personally by other members of the camp. This is a great preventative measure applied to communication that is intended to support each member of the camp and improve the quality of camp life, while also minimizing accidents triggered by miscommunications or misunderstandings. It also boosts camp morale by keeping everyone on the same page, which, believe it or not, is an essential means of survival. A miserable camp makes it hard for people to feel committed to survival because it may seem like there is no point, or they are not gaining anything valuable by living through the emergency. Positive camp morale encourages everyone to keep going for the sake of each other and their own wellbeing.

Tasks 15 to 25: The First Five

The first five, including water, shelter, fire, food, and safety, are essential to your survival, so you are going to need to address and secure the first five for the entire A-Team. You will prepare for the first five ahead of time by setting up measures to protect your A-Team from mild to extreme situations. Then, in active survivalist situations, you will invoke the terms of those measures to ensure that you are actively taking action to secure the first five and survive amid a crisis.

Realize that once you find yourself in an emergency where survival must be secured, this is where you *start*. Ideally, all of your preparedness, assessments, prevention, and communication should be sorted out by now. The only step you may take from previous tasks would be to re-assess the situation based on the present emergency you are facing. This ensures that your A-Team assessments are recent and relevant, you are aware of the state of your current BOHS location, and you are all able to coordinate an effective plan to secure the first five. These initial assessments should be relevant *only* to the securing of the first five. After those have been secured, you can conduct deeper assessments to ensure long-term survival, if that is required.

If you have a particularly large A-Team, or if you have members of the A-Team with special requirements, please ensure that you create a game plan ahead of time. While a survival game plan involving who would do what is important, it is especially important for those who need to secure a large amount of equipment, or may be dealing with special requirements that make securing equipment more challenging. Having a general game plan in advance means you only have to modify that game plan, rather than start from scratch. This saves precious time and ensures you are much quicker and more effective at gathering necessary supplies for survival.

Tasks 26 to 27: Special Equipment

Special equipment is required for most modern humans, and that equipment must be accessed and secured. Keeping individual documents on a thumb drive and a cloud drive, as well as having emergency equipment available for work and/or school, is important. You will need to have all of this organized and set up at all times.

During a dire emergency, special equipment may not seem important. You may think that your work-related or school-related information is irrelevant and that the pressing issue is your survival. Of course, this is true to an extent. Your number one focus should be securing your survival, and the more pressing the emergency, the less likely you will be able to secure these aspects of your survival. However, it is essential to remember that emergencies do eventually end, and society will strive to get back to normal. Attempting to recover your work-related and school-related items, as well as special documents like ID and other necessities, will be much more challenging in a post-emergency situation. This can also elongate your stress and make emotionally recovering from an emergency even more challenging than it already is. Try to remember that life will continue after the emergency, and prepare yourself for that.

Task 28 to 31: Equipment Checklists

Aside from personal equipment, you need your survival equipment. This includes equipment for travel, for your survival vest, for yourself, and your car. You want to have a checklist that defines all of the items required, as well as all of the items on the checklist available in each area and organized at any given time. You should frequently check to make sure everything is there and in stock, that it is in proper working order, and that it has not expired.

Checklists may seem like small, unnecessary aspects of survival. Still, they are essential tools that can make all the difference. A properly-populated checklist serves to remind you of all the items that are essential to survival. Understand that it is nearly impossible to know what you will need in an emergency until you are in one and realize you do not have what you need. Fortunately, enough emergencies have happened by now that other people have recalled their needs and placed them together on well-populated lists served to protect you and your family from lacking an essential item during an emergency. Following these checklists ensures that you have everything you need.

During an active emergency, after you have secured your first five, you may review checklists to ensure you have everything required for short-term and long-term survival situations. This way, if you realize you are missing anything, you can improvise with bush-made tools or other resources so that when that item comes up as needed, you are ready with an alternative.

Tasks 32 to 34: Leaving

The final tasks are relevant to leaving and include having everything pre-packaged and ready to go. This will include having a checklist for GnG Bags that are developed for mild situations, as well as GnG Bags that are developed for moderate to extreme situations. Both bags should always be fully stocked and ready for use, no matter what.

It is essential that you keep all of your survival and emergency equipment prepared inside of GnG bags from the start. Storing them loosely in a closet, garage, or shed may result in you being unable to bring all or any items with you because they were not ready for immediate evacuation. In situations like hurricanes, fires, or earthquakes, immediate evacuation may be required to protect yourself from danger. Ready-packed bags prevents you from having to make the hard choice of risking injury or death or leaving your preparedness items behind during an emergency.

Ensure that you efficiently pack your bags and that you practice carrying them away from the house. It would be incredibly disappointing to realize that your well-packed bags were packed too heavy, or in such a way that makes them impossible to fit into your vehicle upon evacuation. A proper practice run ensures that everything can be reasonably removed from your home and brought with you in a GnG situation.

CHAPTER 5
The 34 Tasks Of Survival

The 34 tasks of survival are done in two phases. The first phase is for you to run through all of these tasks *before* finding yourself in a survival situation so that you are confident that you are prepared for anything that may happen. The second phase is to run through them during an emergency to ensure you are ready to survive that emergency. In moderate to extreme emergencies, you will likely find that there is first the next phase of survival, which is to protect yourself against whatever is coming. That may not be entirely possible for you to plan, as you cannot anticipate when a crisis will strike, so you are going to have to think on your toes and do what is right at that moment. For example, in an earthquake, it would not be wise to immediately run back to your IRP or ERP and begin executing your tasks. Instead, you will first need to survive the earthquake; then, you will need to start taking action on the immediate follow-up. Since there is no way to prepare for exactly what you will do in the very moment crisis strikes, you need to educate yourself and trust in your skill when it comes to surviving that initial strike. Immediately after the initial crisis has struck, however, you need to jump into action with your survival plan.

Ensure that you complete each task entirely before moving on to the next one. As well, learn how to execute the task or use any relevant tools in case of an emergency. For example, task 28 reflects travel equipment. You need to know how to collect and store your travel equipment, as well as how to use it so that when you need it, you are familiar with how it works. Practice runs should be performed with your A-Team, too, to ensure you are all on the same page.

It would be wise to keep a copy of this task list available in a printed format in your GnG Bag, as well so that when you get into the bush, you can look through it and refresh yourself.

Sometimes, no matter how well you educate yourself, a state of emergency can prevent your memory from functioning correctly, and having vital information written down can support you with recalling everything that needs to be done.

Task 1: A-Team Contacts

Having a contact sheet on hand is crucial when it comes to survival. You want your A-Team Contacts list to include contact information for every person on your A-Team, including yourself, as well as important numbers to know. This includes the numbers for doctors and specialists for each member of the A-Team, poison control numbers, emergency contact numbers, work and school numbers, and insurance and personal identification numbers. These numbers ensure that anyone can immediately be contacted in case of an emergency. Every member of the A-Team should have a copy. You should also have one in your GnG bags so that they can be accessed quickly when you are away from home.

Task 2: Water Bottles

Even in a short term emergency, you are going to need to have water available to sustain yourself. A lack of access to water can rapidly become an emergency in and of itself. You should have two quarts of water per person in your house, which would create enough water for six days for each person. The water should be kept clean, filtered, and stored in a way that is easy to access and easy to transport. While canned water kept in glass canning jars may last longer than those kept in plastic, keep in mind the glass adds weight when it comes to transporting. Stainless steel canteens are a great alternative to glass as they remain sterile, will not leach chemicals into the water, and are much more lightweight when transporting. Plus, canteens can be worn around your neck, which can free up space inside of the GnG bag.

Task 3: First Aid Kit

A well-stocked first-aid kit should be essential for any household. They are useful for treating everyday injuries at home, and they can be lifesaving in certain emergency situations. Stock your first aid kit with standard first aid items, as well as items unique to your family's medical needs. If you know that a certain family member is prone to something, in particular, stock up on extra supplies for that particular ailment. For example, if a family member is prone to excessive bleeding, keep additional gauze and bandages on hand in case they sustain an injury.

Every first aid kit should have:

- Emergency phone numbers and important personal contacts
- Safety pins
- Tweezers
- Scissors
- Instant ice packs
- Latex gloves (disposable) or neoprene gloves if you have a latex allergy
- Flashlight with extra batteries that are stored in a separate bag
- Sterile gauze pads in small and large squares for dressing wounds
- Self-adhesive tape and adhesive medical tape
- Roller bandages and triangle bandages for keeping injured limbs in place
- Adhesive bandages in an assortment of sizes
- Antiseptic wipes and soap
- Pencil and paper
- Thermometer
- Pocket mask or face shield

- CPR mask
- Emergency blanket
- Eye patches
- Coins for a payphone and cash in small bills
- Drugs like ibuprofen, naproxen, and acetaminophen for pain, and diphenhydramine for minor allergic reactions
- Medications that are unique to the people the first aid kit will be serving, such as specific drugs, inhalers, epi-pens, insulin, and other necessary supplies
- A first aid manual

If you have a family member who is prone to bleeding, or if you are going into an area where lacerations could occur, and you will not have access to immediate medical support, you may also keep a diaper or a few feminine pads in your first aid kit. These are made of clean, absorbent material that can absorb a large amount of blood without having to be removed. This means you can apply consistent pressure for longer with them.

Task 4: Check Status of A-Team

The fourth task for survival is to check the status of your A-Team. If you are in the preparation phase, you will pay attention to more long term and average conditions. At the same time, if you are in survival mode, you will check for more recent, present, and pressing issues.

During the preparation phase, you should compile a "profile" of each member of the A-Team. This profile should include that person's age, date of birth, and overall health. Consider overall physical condition, including their weight and strength, as well as how easy it is (or isn't) for them to perform more physical tasks such as walking or running. Also, take note of their medical status, any allergies they may have, and any medications they may be on. Consider any special needs they may have, as well as their ability to engage in specific tasks that are related to survival such as swimming, driving, splitting wood, carrying things, and so forth. Lastly, consider what type of access they have to vehicles.

You should prepare your survival plan to ensure that each member of the A-Team's needs will be met accordingly. As well, plan for plenty of room for necessities to be packed, and consider their abilities and needs when locating your BOHS and delegating duties. Make sure any tasks delegated to each member of the A-Team are duties they can reasonably handle and allow them to maintain those duties.

Review all status profiles and designations of each A-Team member before engaging in any survival situation. You need to know that you have up-to-date information on their health, wellness, energy, abilities, and needs. You also need to be confident that any tasks delegated to this individual are tasks that they will reasonably be able to assume and complete while you are in a survivalist situation. While everyone needs to pull their weight, your survival camp will run best if everyone is tasked with something that is within their ability as it ensures that the job will get done right and that there will be minimal chance of running into injuries or illnesses along the way.

Task 5: Area Study

An area study happens over three parts, and it will be used to help your A-Team prepare a plan for survival. The first part of the task is to study your general geography, the second part of the task is to study your BOHS location, and the third part of the task is to review the area of the BOHS location once you arrive in a survival situation.

Studying your general geography is important as it allows you to know what to expect in the area where you will be surviving. This study should include a study of the landscape, vegetation, animals, and likely threats in your area. Keep yourself updated and knowledgeable in these things so you can use it to your advantage in any survival situation. You must expand your studies to your entire geographical location and not just the area of your BOHS, as you never know when an emergency could make your BOHS inaccessible or unusable. This way, if your BOHS fails, you can find an alternative and still feel confident surviving in that area.

Studying your BOHS location before a real emergency hits is a good idea as it allows you to understand the geography immediately surrounding the BOHS. During this study, you want to locate everything you learned from your general geography study of your area and use that to your advantage. Find water, the best areas for trapping, and the best locations for shelter.

Reviewing your BOHS location in a survival situation only requires a mild area study. At this point, you already know the region quite well based on your previous studies, so you simply need an updated view on what is going on and what the best methods for navigation and survival would be in this area. This allows you to recognize any changes that may have occurred, refresh yourself on anything you learned previously, and ultimately familiarize yourself with the area. It will be a lot easier for you to survive in a familiar setting than it will for you to survive in a foreign one, so take this task seriously. In a familiar setting, you are aware of what is normal. Therefore it becomes easier to spot abnormalities or potential threats caused by the geography or the local wildlife. In a foreign setting, you are not entirely aware of what to expect, and therefore it becomes more challenging to spot normal from abnormal and to protect yourself against geography and wildlife.

Task 6: Firearm Prevention

Firearms are imperative to survival situations, especially ones where you will be residing in the bush. A gun will protect you against wildlife and intruders and keep you safe from anything that may be going on in your area. With that being said, guns must be used and stored safely to prevent any accidental injuries or deaths from occurring. Every single gun should have a safety on it. That safety should be secured in place anytime the gun is not actively being used. This safety should be applied when the gun is being stored, as well as when it is being carried.

Your day to day dwelling, as well as your BOHS, should both have locations for you to safely store your guns so that they are inaccessible to anyone but yourself or those who have the code to your safe. Keeping your guns in these safes anytime they are not in use is crucial to avoid accidental injury or death.

The next method of prevention you need to consider with guns is preventing injury or death by teaching everyone how to use them safely. Knowing how to safely use a gun prevents direct injury from the gun itself or injury from a failure to use the gun for protection. To put it simply, if you cannot aim and stop the attacker, you will end up being attacked. Everyone on the A-Team should learn how to safely load, aim, and shoot a gun, as well as what to do with the gun after. Target practice is also a good idea and should be completed at least once per week at the camp during a survival situation to ensure that everyone has a strong aim and is able to safely protect themselves in case of an emergency.

Task 7: Fire Prevention

Fire prevention needs to be practiced at home, as well as at your survival site. Fire prevention at home can be accomplished with smoke alarms, escape routes, and fire extinguishers. You should also be sure not to leave any small appliances plugged in or left on, especially when you are away from home. As well, keep flammable materials away from heat sources and open flames, and do your part in preventing fires.

At camp, fire prevention can be accomplished by keeping fires properly contained and safely away from fuel sources. They should also be kept away from low hanging branches, dry brush, and your shelter, as a fire can quickly jump over and start burning everything around it. Every single fire should be put out when it is not being monitored or in use, to ensure that it is not able to cause uncontrolled burning. Take extra precautions when lighting a fire to keep you warm through the night. Keep the area free of debris, carefully block it with rocks to prevent it blowing out of the fire pit, and stay far enough away that it does not accidentally catch your sleeping bag or supplies on fire.

Should a fire break out, you will need something on hand to help put it out. At home, flour and fire extinguishers are great. In the bush, dirt and water are great. Flour or dirt should be used on grease and alcohol fires, as water will only worsen the fire. On all other fires, fire extinguishers and water are fine. If you do not know what caused the fire, use something to smother it, or get far away from the fire as quickly as possible. If you are at home, call for help. If you are in the bush and not presently afraid of the authorities, you should call for help in that scenario, too. Keep the emergency numbers for fire on hand at all times so that you can quickly call if needed.

Task 8: Drowning Prevention

Drowning is a serious risk for death, whether you realize it or not. An average of 332 people die per year from accidental drownings. While that may not seem like much, the risk is drastically increased if the person is particularly young, or if they are unfit and in an emergency situation. At home, youths, particularly toddlers and younger, are at highest risk for drowning. Elders or those who may have a condition such as narcolepsy can be high at risk, too, if they take a bath and find themselves suddenly submerged and unable to get out. Weak swimmers are especially endangered in survival situations where you may need to survive near large bodies of water or rapidly moving rivers.

At home, drowning prevention can be accomplished by avoiding allowing anyone who is particularly young, elderly, or ill with certain conditions to be around bodies of water without supervision or proper safety measures in place. The young should always be supervised, period. Those who are elderly or who have medical conditions can be protected by having proper seats installed in their tubs and rails to make getting in and out much easier.

In a survival situation, you must be prepared to look for all possible risks of drowning and then prevent them in whatever ways possible. If anyone on the A-Team is not a strong swimmer, either avoid crossing water altogether, look for alternate routes, or look for shallow areas where they can walk across. Avoid camping out near any fast-moving, deep, or rough bodies of water. As well, avoid ever putting your back to the water when you are at the top of a cliff or bank on the body of dangerous waters, as one misstep could lead you right off the edge.

Task 9: Poison Prevention

Poison prevention is another prevention practice that needs to be done both at home and in camp. At home, the most common culprits for poisonings are cleaning supplies and contaminated water or foods. In the bush, poisoning commonly comes from what you drink or consume.

At home, always be extremely careful when dealing with chemicals, especially those that are in cleaning solutions. You must be cautious about exposure by minimizing or eliminating a cleaning solution's contact with your skin, eyes, and mouth. You should avoid ever consuming any, either purposefully or accidentally, such as by accidentally spraying food on the counter while you are cleaning and then later eating the food. You should avoid inhaling too many of the fumes. In some cases, you need to avoid inhaling any fumes, period. You also need to prevent anyone in your family, especially young kids who would not know better, from accessing these solutions to avoid accidental poisonings in children.

At home, *never* mix the following solutions as they can be fatal:

- Bleach and vinegar should never be mixed as they create chlorine gas, which, even at low levels, can cause respiratory damage.
- Bleach and ammonia should never be mixed as they create chloramine, which can also cause respiratory damage often to fatal degrees.
- Different drain cleaners (even from the same brand) should never be mixed because when they are combined can explode based on the chemicals in them. If you have recently treated a sink, do not treat it again later with a different product, instead call a plumber and let them know what you used.
- Hydrogen peroxide and vinegar may be mixed on surfaces but should never be stored mixed in the same container. Together, they create peracetic acid, which can be toxic and can irritate your eyes, skin, and respiratory system.
- Bleach and rubbing alcohol should never be mixed because they produce chloroform, which can be extremely irritating, toxic, and can cause you to pass out.

Be especially careful with cleaning products that are named after a brand and not the chemical within them. Not knowing what is in the cleaning solutions you are using can lead to you accidentally creating fatal mixes of chemicals. For example, many window cleaning solutions contain ammonia, so if you cleaned your windows and then immediately started cleaning a surface with bleach, you could create chloramine in the air, which could cause you to pass out. Anyone using household cleaners should always be old enough to do so, and knowledgeable enough to do so safely. Store them up high and locked away from anyone who should not be touching them.

At camp, you must be aware of poisonous plants, poisonous and venomous animals, and potential contaminants in water. Avoiding plants and animals and thoroughly filtering and purifying your water will prevent you from becoming endangered through either type of exposure. It is advised that you take time to identify local poison threats and keep a detailed list, with pictures if possible, laminated and present in your GnG bag so that when you reach your BOHS location, you have this available. That way, your list is relevant to your area and easy for you and everyone on the A-Team to understand and follow. Activated charcoal is always good to have on hand as you can pump someone's system to hopefully remove poison from someone's body, in case of accidental ingestion. If venomous animals are common in your area, learn the appropriate protocol to extract venom from bites. This way, any bites can be promptly treated.

Task 10: Environmental Danger Assessment and Prevention

Environmental dangers can be a severe threat to your wellbeing. In the bush, they are called widowmakers. You need to be prepared to assess for danger and prevent that risk from becoming a severe issue at any point so long as you are around it.

At home, you need to be aware of what your possible environmental dangers look like based on the geographical area that you live in, such as tornadoes, hurricanes, earthquakes, wildfires, or avalanches. While these threats are not going to occur every single day, they can develop rapidly. Knowing how to monitor for them will ensure that you are prepared if the threat of a natural disaster arises.

In the bush, you need to survey your survival area to identify any potential threats that may be present quickly. Avoid writing any threats off as being "unlikely" and instead honestly assess every possible danger right down to the last possible thing. Consider how you will prevent those dangers from harming anyone. Staying away from dangerous cliffs, monitoring possibly risky logs, and knowing how you will protect yourself and each other from local wildlife, will all keep you safe.

Task 11: Man-Made Danger Assessment and Prevention

The last assessment and prevention check that needs to be completed is the man-made danger assessment and prevention.

At home, man-made threats linger inside of your house in the form of natural gas lines, faulty wiring, poor building techniques, and other such issues. Outside, man-made threats can include dams, traffic, and even people bearing firearms in certain areas. You also want to be aware of things such as chemical plants, the government, or authoritarian figures who may be taking advantage of their authority, down electric wires, and even nearby drug houses where they may be cooking illegal drugs or chemicals. All of these types of threats can pose a threat to your safety and wellbeing, so they should be assessed, monitored, and addressed in terms of how you will prevent them from causing any direct threat to you, your family, or the A-Team. You should also have a plan for how you will proceed if the threat level increases.

In the bush, man-made dangers could include hydro dams or other man-made structures. These can be highly dangerous and should be avoided at all costs to avoid the looming threat. Other man-made dangers can be made from people right in your camp.

People swinging axes, carrying or shooting guns, fires, and even poorly designed building structures can be a risk. It is vital always to pause, assess any possible dangers of a situation beforehand, and proceed accordingly. Never use hazardous tools around other people without knowing where those other people are and knowing that they are aware of you using the device. Never carry, fell, or drop heavy items when you do not know where other people are. Be sure to double-check structures to ensure they are not at risk of falling or caving in. Also, make sure campfires are far enough away from the structure that you are not risking them being caught on fire.

Task 12: Map and Navigation Supplies

In an urban setting, relying on internet-based navigation systems or digital navigation systems is easy. You can turn them on through your cell phone or through devices that you set up in your car, or that are built into your car, and reliably follow them anywhere you need to go. In the bush, navigating is not quite so easy. Most internet-based or digital navigation systems will not work. If they do, they will eventually die and become unusable. You must have other means of navigation to protect yourself in the bush.

Navigation tools you should have include a detailed map of your destination, a compass, a pedometer, and markers you can use to mark your path. Ensure that you know how to use these tools and navigation techniques such as handrails, backstops, baselines, aiming off, and panic azimuths, so you can safely navigate your location. Each of these methods is described in *Survival 101: Bushcraft* and should be well-understood and used by everyone on the A-Team to ensure that everyone stays safe and easy to locate in the bush.

Task 13: Emergency Radio

Emergency radios are critical to have on hand and should be kept nearby at all times. Your emergency radio can be useful both at home and in the bush. A proper emergency radio should be one that can be powered by a hand crank. This ensures that if you run out of battery power or batteries, or if the battery compartment somehow becomes damaged, you can still charge the radio. One way radios and two-way radios are essential, depending on what emergency you are in.

One way radios are radios that allow people to listen to emergency messages through radio frequencies in the case of an event. They are frequently used by authorities to inform the public on looming and active threats such as storms or devastating earthquakes. Keeping your emergency radio on hand will allow you to hear live updates as the threat continues. Updates will often tell you what to do, how to stay safe, and when it is safe to come out of hiding.

Two-way radios are important in the bush as they can help you stay in contact with people who are in the bush with you. Be sure to get two-way radios that can be solar-powered and that have the most extended range possible. This way, they can be used from great distances, and you do not have to worry about charging the radios when you go out.

Task 14: A-Team Codewords

A-Team codewords are a benefit to have for two different reasons. First and foremost, code words can make talking to each other more efficient, and this can offer a range of benefits. In a dangerous situation, a single codeword is easier to say than an entire sentence, and it is easier to hear, too. For example, in a hospital, code blue means an adult is in cardiac arrest. Having a quick codeword indicates that you do not have to attempt to describe the situation through yelling or through a two-way radio, and people will be able to recognize the level of emergency and respond accordingly quickly. These codes can also be useful when hunting, as they can be whispered into radios or called to each other from a distance without alerting the animal to your presence. When hunting, short and quick codewords avoid alerting the animal, you are hunting that you are present. When hunting, there should be codewords used to indicate the presence of an animal and to indicate when someone is going to shoot an animal. This way, everyone knows where to look, and they can stay clear of the animal to avoid an accidental injury.

A-Team words are also helpful in situations where you may not necessarily trust the government or outsiders, and where outsiders may pose a threat. Like speaking in your language, code words can allow you to communicate specific information without outsiders knowing what you are talking about. If you are in a situation that is threatening and involves other people, this is a good way to avoid the others from knowing what you are talking about.

In some situations, you may not necessarily be able to talk out loud, but you may still need to communicate. Code signals or body languages, then, are excellent choices for these situations. In intimate settings, a particular finger or hand signal or even a signal with the face can send a particular piece of information. From distances, certain arm movements or leg movements or even poses with the entire body could convey certain pieces of information. Be sure that everyone on the A-Team knows exactly what the code words are and how to use them so that everyone is able to communicate clearly. As well, avoid creating too many and instead only use a necessary few. Review the code words regularly until everyone clearly remembers them in case of an emergency. This way, no one is left trying to recall what a certain code means or finds themselves misinterpreting it and exposing themselves to danger.

Task 15: Rotation and Inspection Checklist

To remain prepared for any emergency, you need to know that everything required for your survival is available at any given time. Being prepared means that you not only have everything put together and checklists are in place, but that you regularly go through these items to ensure that everything is still prepared for your survival in case of an emergency. This is one thing many beginner preppers forget to do, and what ends up happening is they find themselves in an emergency situation, only to realize that most of their gear has expired or is no longer in working order due to not having been used for so long. While it is great to know that you don't often need your survival gear, it would be a tragedy to need it and not have access to it because you have allowed it to expire or seize in storage.

Your rotation and inspection checklist should require you to periodically check through each of the 34 tasks to ensure that everything is prepared, and you know how to use it. You should also have a checklist that runs through all of the equipment you are to keep on hand so that you can go through it and check in on all of your gear, as well.

Every six months, you should go through your rotation and inspection checklists. Any food or consumable items that are coming up to expiry should be removed, used in everyday life, and promptly replaced with fresh materials. Thoroughly test all tools, items, and objects to ensure that all of the parts are working. Any broken gear should be removed from your kit and immediately replaced. *You are not done with the inspection until everything has been restored and in proper working order.* Be as prompt as you can about returning such things to avoid finding yourself in a situation where you have forgotten to return something and find yourself without it in an emergency situation.

Task 16: Water for Mild Emergency

Water for mild emergencies should be enough to last you up to 2 days. Bottled water works, though you need to be prepared to replace them every one to two years to prevent plastic from breaking down and contaminating your water. If you prefer, you can keep a 5-gallon jug on hand or even can your water in glass jars, which tends to last longer since glass will not break down into the water. You will, however, need to maintain canned water. Over the years, some of it will naturally disappear, so you may need to redo those jars to ensure that they are full. Then, every 30 years, you are going to want to completely throw out all of the water and replace your cans lids, as they can start to rust, which can contaminate your water.

Two days of water for every person in your household, plus a bit extra is always ideal for mild emergencies. This way, if you find yourself in a situation where you cannot go out and get water, you have plenty of access. You will want to set aside 1 gallon of water per day, per person. You should also store enough for any pets in your household. This water needs to be safe enough to consume, but will also be used for other means such as brushing your teeth. So, let's say you have a family of four plus two dogs, you would need 6 gallons of water per day or 12 gallons of water for a two-day emergency.

Task 17: Water for Moderate to Extreme Emergency

For moderate to extreme emergencies, you need enough water for six days for everyone in your home. You will also need a means for filtering more water in case six days of water is not enough. Let's start by focusing on the six days of water for each person in your house. Again, you will need one gallon of water per day, per person, as well as water for your pets. So, if you are a family of four with two dogs, you would need six gallons of water per day or thirty-six gallons of water for six days. Thirty-six gallons of water would be 144 x 2-quart jars, or 7 x 5-gallon jugs plus a few water bottles to make up for the extra gallon. *Or* you could invest in water barrels. High-density polyethylene (HDPE) plastic water gallons are excellent for storing water in. One can store up to 55 gallons of water, which would exceed your daily usage needs by 19 gallons, or three extra days for a family of four humans and two pets. These extra days can be useful, so do not discredit this option just because it may be larger than your needs.

In addition to having extra water storage available, you should also have a means of filtering water. Toting 55-gallons of water into the bush would be virtually impossible, so you will want to fill your canteens out of the container and bring along as many canteens as you could reasonably carry. Then, you would have a filter or two available, which would allow you to clean your water in the bush. This way, you can fetch water from natural sources and purify it so that it is safe for you to consume or use on your body or in your cleaning rituals in the bush.

There are two types of filters you can use in the bush. Manual filters act like a strainer and allow you to pour your water through, and they purify your water in the process. Purifying drops or tablets are dropped into water, and they purify your water as they dissolve. You should have both available for an emergency so that you can clean your water for an extended period. Make sure you get filters that are intended for natural purposes, as standard filters that purify tap water will not suffice. Tap water has already been treated by water management crews in the city, which means your water filters for the faucet or the fridge further purify and essentially improve the flavor. Purifiers for natural water sources are much more advanced, and they can kill off all of the bacteria, viruses, and parasites that would typically be treated by water management crews in the city.

Task 18: Shelter for Mild Emergency

For a mild emergency, you want to make sure you have access to adequate shelter. Your house is plenty enough for shelter for a mild emergency; however, you should also have backup plans in case your shelter is not accessible or usable during the case of an emergency. With that, there are two levels of preparedness that need to occur for shelter for mild emergencies.

The first level is preparing your own home. It should be in proper working order and should be available for you to live in for up to two weeks without needing anything at any given time. You should have adequate clothes, bedding, cleaning supplies, hygiene products, toiletries, and so forth for two weeks. You should also have adequate money to pay for two weeks of living expenses without any incoming funds so that if you find yourself unable to work due to a mild emergency, you can afford to pay for your shelter and all necessary bills associated with your shelter.

The second level of preparedness is to prepare for where you will go if your home is not an option. You should know of at least one friend or family member that you can stay with in case of an emergency. Everyone in your household should see which friend or family member's house will be the designated emergency shelter. They should also know the address and the way to get there so that if everyone is not together when an emergency strikes, everyone still knows where to go so they can safely gather following the emergency.

Task 19: Shelter for Moderate to Extreme Emergency

In moderate to extreme situations, you need to have accelerated plans on how you are going to survive. You need to know where you are going to go and how that shelter is going to work for your survival. There are two options for moderate or extreme emergencies: city allocated shelters or the bush for survival in the wilderness.

Note that if you end up in a city allocated shelter or shelter that the municipality opens up during emergencies. You are not going to have full control over how you spend your time or how you contribute to your survival. In these settings, authorities will have an emergency response plan in place, and you will have to follow what they have told you to do. However, in some cases, this may be the safest course of action.

If you end up having to retreat to the bush for shelter, you are going to need to have everything on hand for survival in these situations. This includes having a BOHS location determined ahead of time, as well as all of the navigation and survival tools you will need to survive. You will need tarps, a tent if possible, ropes, stakes, ground cloth, and an ax to help create your shelter. Even if you have a pre-built shelter such as a cabin in the woods, you should still have tools on hand to create a shelter in case, for some reason, your cabin is not able to be inhabited.

In addition to all of the shelter items, make sure you have everything you need to sleep comfortably. Sleeping bags, blankets, and sleeping clothes should all be available so that you can keep yourself warm and protected during the night hours.

Task 20: Fire for Mild Emergency

Fire is responsible for both core temperature and for cooking food over in case of an emergency. If the electricity goes out, for example, a fire will allow you to keep yourself warm and continue to cook your food as usual. In a mild emergency setting, such as a down powerline or a temporary outage, you will need a way to warm yourself and your family and prepare meals for yourself at home. While a home may be more comfortable, fire can be more difficult to manage safely in urban settings.

There are three ways that you can safely bring fire indoors for warmth and cooking. They include fireplaces or wood-burning stoves, gas ranges, and candles. Fireplaces or wood-burning stoves can contain fires just as you would in the bush, which means they are incredibly useful. You will need to keep your chimney clean at all times, however, to avoid becoming poisoned by the gasses from the fireplace. If you have a gas oven or gas range, you can continue to use the elements on that range, too. Simply turn on the element and use a barbecue lighter to light the element, which will cause the gas to ignite. With gas ranges, the only part that is "off" in an outage is the electricity that powers the ignitor, and you can do that manually. Do make sure, however, that you only start it on low to avoid flame shooting out in all directions, and that you inspect gas lines for leakage before lighting any fires near your range. If there is a leakage, not only should you not light a fire but also evacuate immediately as the leak rapidly becomes fatal. For candles, you can burn as many candles as you can reasonably supervise in your home. Kerosene lamps and lanterns are also great for indoors.

Outside of your home, you can use barbecues or barbecue pits to have a fire. These are great for warming up, as well as for cooking over. Be sure to keep extra propane, charcoal blocks, or wood chips on hand so that you always have fuel for your fire. Smokers are also excellent for cooking meat if you have one, plus if you find yourself in a long term emergency, they can be used to cure meats, so they don't spoil.

Task 21: Fire for Moderate to Extreme Emergency

In moderate to extreme emergencies, you will be likely to have to procure fire outdoors. Knowing how to build and maintain a fire is crucial as it will allow you to keep yourself warm and give yourself something to cook safely. Fire crafting will require you to have a combustion tool such as a lighter or matches, access to fire starters, and fuel to supply your fire. You will also need somewhere to build it. If you are in an urban setting, fire starters can be the lint from your dryer, ripped up pieces of cardboard tubes, or cotton balls. In the wilderness, dry brush and grass, dry leaves, and pinecones are great fire starters. Fuel will virtually always be some form of dry wood, though new wood split off of a fresh tree will work in a pinch; however, you will have to be careful not to add too much, or it will drown out your fire.

There are countless fire lays you can use outdoors, though I am going to teach you the two which are most accessible and will get you furthest. These include the teepee fire lay and the Dakota pit fire lay. For either fire, you will start by cleaning off space on the ground where you can build a fire without it catching dry materials off the ground and spreading out of control. You can also shape out a fire pit using rocks, if you wish, to help contain your fire.

The teepee fire lay is created by placing fire-starting materials in the very center of your fire pit. Then, you will use kindling sized log cuts to make a small teepee over the starting materials. Do not make the teepee too dense, or oxygen will not get through and let your fire start. Next, create a giant teepee over the smaller teepee using most massive split logs or branches, which will serve as your fuel. Again, do not make them too dense, or the oxygen will not get through for your fire. Now, start the starting materials in the center. They will catch on fire, then they will catch the smaller kindling on fire, and then that will start your fuel logs going.

The Dakota pit fire lay uses two holes in the ground, and it is ideal for cooking, as well as for keeping a fire going in a windy area. You will create the Dakota fire pit by digging a small hole into the ground at least 1' deep. Then, you will dig another hole into the ground on an angle aimed at the bottom of the original hole. Do not break through with the shovel, though. Use your hand to break a hole through the bottom that is roughly the size of your fist. Now, layer starting materials in the bottom of the central hole and make a small teepee shape out of kindling over the top of the starting materials. Start the starting materials on fire, then allow them to burn up into the kindling. You should get a pretty good fire going in your pit in no time. The secondary hole will feed oxygen into your fire, keeping it going. When you add fuel logs to your fire, make sure they are relatively small so that plenty of oxygen can still get in and around your fire.

Task 22: Food for Mild Emergency

For a mild emergency, you want to have enough food on hand for at least two weeks at any given time. This means that you should seek to stock your pantry with enough staples that you will have two weeks' worth of food stored *on top of* your average grocery shopping routine. Choose ready to eat, non-perishable food items such as canned foods or pre-packaged foods that can be cooked right away. Homemade canned goods work great, too. Ensure they are prepared properly, though, to avoid the risk of contracting botulism due to poorly preserved food. Also, choose to have pantry staples on hand that allow you to cook and bake things such as soups, bread, and other meal items. The freezer is another great place to store items, but be careful not to rely exclusively on it. If your power goes out, the contents of your freezer would be rendered useless fairly quickly. If you do have food in your freezer, be sure to have a plan for how you will use it rapidly in case something happens to your freezer. Keeping extra tools on hand for preserving foods is a good idea. You can smoke and dry excess meat and properly can fruits and vegetables out of the freezer should it become unreliable. This way, you can salvage as much as possible.

Keeping up to two weeks' worth of food on hand means that in an emergency, you have plenty of food to eat. A great example of a usage for this store would be for emergencies such as the new coronavirus. When coronavirus first hit, there was a strain on our food sources. However, many items were still available in limited quantities. Having food reserves ensures that should this happen again; you have access to what you need during that period.

Task 23: Food for Moderate to Extreme Emergency

For a moderate to an extreme emergency, you want to have food that will last you at least one month. However, many preppers argue that you should have enough staples for anywhere from 3 months to 12 months, depending on what they believe is likely going to happen. You should find the amount that feels comfortable for you and store that amount. However, it should be no less than one month's worth of food in your pantry at any given time. Again, this should be on top of your regular grocery shopping, and it should contain items that are ready to eat, as well as ingredients for greater recipes.

It is also essential that you consider your needs for food in case you have to evacuate your house. Keep some food inside your GnG bag at all times, and be prepared to add extras from your pantry if you have to evacuate in an emergency. For your GnG bag, meals that are kept in vacuum-sealed bags or pouches are ideal as they will be lightest to carry. Canned items are good as well, but stay away from most things in glass jars as these jars can break in the bag and destroy your items.

A proper trapping kit, fishing kit, and game processing tools should be in your GnG bag, too. This way, you have everything you need to harvest food when you are in the wilderness. A book about edible plants and dangerous plants in your locale would be ideal. This will also help you safely forage for vegetation so that you are not relying solely on meat in the bush. You should also have a detailed guide on how to butcher, cook, and preserve small mammals, medium mammals, birds, reptiles and amphibians, and fish in the bush. I discuss all of those details in *Survival 101: Bushcraft*.

Task 24: First Aid for Mild Emergency

First aid is essential in emergencies. Some situations become emergencies solely because someone has become ill or injured, so having proper first aid supplies on hand can help you deal with that situation. You should have a properly stocked first aid kit on hand at all times, and everyone in your house and on your A-Team should know how to use the contents of that kit.

For mild emergencies, a first aid kit should also be kept in any vehicles you own, as well as anywhere that you may frequent, such as your place of work. If you are dropping your child off somewhere such as a daycare facility on a regular basis or with a family member or friend to be watched, make sure they also have a properly stocked first aid kit for minor emergencies.

Task 25: First Aid for Moderate to Extreme Emergency

For moderate to extreme emergency situations, you need properly stocked first aid kits on hand as well as education on how to use those kits, and how to administer basic first aid support.

First, let's talk about the first aid kits you will need. You want a fully stocked first aid kit with enough supplies in it for every single person on the A-Team for your BOHS location. Then, you want smaller first aid kits that can be carried away from camp, and that should be carried away from camp *any* time someone leaves camp. This means if you leave camp to go to the cooking location, the food storage location, to get water, to go set traps, or to do anything else, you bring this first aid kit with you. The on the go first aid kit should include tools for cleaning and dressing wounds, as well as for securing broken digits or limbs. Everything else can stay back at camp.

Everyone on the A-Team should also take a first aid course to learn how to administer first aid on the scene if need be. This will help you treat yourself and treat other members of the A-Team should something go wrong. Understanding how to administer basic first aid will result in you knowing how to handle minor wounds, set broken digits or limbs, and rescue and resuscitate people. First aid courses will also educate everyone on how to safely assess dangerous situations so that they can rescue an individual without putting themselves in harm's way.

Task 26: Emergency Equipment for Work/School

Emergency equipment for work or school includes any equipment one might need to be able to complete their duty away from work or school. This is more common in mild emergencies, as more advanced emergencies would not likely allow you to continue working or completing school work as you went. For mild emergencies, however, having access to the tools you need to continue working will ensure that you can continue earning an income and that your child is able to continue advancing their education as you endure your emergency.

Task 27: Digital Copies of Important Documents

Important documents like ID, birth certificates, marriage certificates, social security numbers, insurance numbers and papers, and health ID numbers should always be kept on hand. Bank numbers, investment numbers, and other important documents should also be kept available. With that being said, the hard copies of these documents can become damaged, so you will want to keep them available in digital copies, too. To create digital copies of your important documents, be sure to upload them by scanning them to your computer. Then, e-mail them to yourself and keep them on at least two separate USB drives kept in 2 separate places. One should be in your GnG bag; the other should be kept away from the house, such as in a safety deposit box. This ensures that you always have a copy of your important documents, no matter what happens. In emergency situations, these documents are very important, so you will want to be confident that you have them, and that you know where they are.

Task 28: Travel Equipment

When preparing for a survival situation, it is important that you don't get caught up on your place of origin and your destination and forget entirely about your mode of transportation! If you will need to leave your home for survival, or if you will be away from your home and need to return, you need to have equipment on hand for traveling with. Keeping some equipment in your GnG bag, as well as in your car, is a great way to make sure that you have everything you need to travel with. If you do not have a car, keep extra cash on hand so that you can pay for transportation if need be, in more mild emergencies.

Your GnG bag should include the following travel equipment: a pair of comfortable hiking boots, a change of dry clothes, a flashlight, and extra bags to make hauling your supplies easier. If you are heading to a place with mild terrain, consider a folding wagon that can be used on back road trails, as this will take some of the weight off your back and help you get more into your camp.

Another thing to consider as far as travel equipment goes is having a travel plan. In other words, how will all members of the A-Team be traveling in an emergency situation? Which cars will be taken, who will be responsible for driving who, and how will you assign travel to each individual? Knowing where everyone will be traveling, and how, ensures that everyone is accounted for in the plan. This way, you know everyone will arrive at the BOHS safely.

Task 29: Survival Vest Equipment

Survival vests are a type of survival gear that is worn on your body and that are designed to help keep you warm, dry, and comfortable while also allowing you to bring gear along with you easily. Survival vests have multiple pockets and compartments for storing things in. The benefit of having a well-stocked vest is that you do not have to open your bag and search for things every time you are looking for something that you would commonly need on the trail. As well, if you are going to be surviving in the bush for a while, you can often carry everything you need for shorter trips in your vest and only take a few small things with you in a pack or your hands.

Your vest should always have:

- A fishing kit
- Survival blankets, an emergency blanket, and small tarps
- Map, compass, and flashlight
- Tough trash bag
- Dental floss and needles
- Small first aid kit and sanitizer
- Water purification tablets or drops
- Duct tape and cordage
- Firestarter and a lighter
- Whistle and signal mirror
- Multi-tool and knife
- Small cook pot and power bars
- Survival poncho

Task 30: Personal Equipment

Personal equipment includes everything that one person needs for survival. Since you have already addressed water, food, shelter, fire, and first aid, the next thing to address is your personal needs. Personal needs include things like clothes, toothbrushes and toothpaste, personal medications, and other personal needs you might have. If you have a child in your house, you might have a particular blanket for that child or a special stuffed animal you use to help comfort them. If you have someone who particularly likes reading, you might include a book or two in your pack if you have room, so they have something to do. While there is not a lot of downtime in the bush, having something to keep you occupied in a positive manner, such as reading or a game or pocket chess, can help keep your mind calm. This is a great way to distract yourself if you are having a hard time mentally processing the stress of being in a survival situation.

Task 31: Car Equipment

In your car, you should also have basic equipment to help you repair your car if need be. A spare tire plus everything needed to change your tire should be kept on hand, in the car, at all times. As well, flares, cones, a reflective safety jacket, extra motor oil and coolant, an emergency blanket, and a flashlight with extra batteries are all crucial to have in your car at all times. A travel-sized tool kit would also be ideal, particularly if it has screwdrivers, an adjustable wrench, pliers, and a pocket knife. Lastly, keep jumper cables on hand, which will help you jumpstart your car if need be. As well, keep your tank as close to empty at all times so that if you ever do come across an emergency, you have enough gas to get you where you need to go.

Task 32: Pre-Packaged Supplies

Pre-packaged supplies include anything you can purchase that has already been designed for you, essentially. Bushcraft and survival stores often sell kits that contain everything you need for certain aspects of living in the wilderness. For example, there may be cooking kits, personal hygiene kits, burn kits, first aid kits, fishing kits, and other such kits pre-built. These kits are excellent as they tend to come at a discounted price, are already packaged in a way that makes them easy to transport, and are often kept organized. Ensure that any pre-packaged kits have everything you need in them. Do not be afraid to add extra things to a kit if need be so that you have everything you feel you would need in a survival setting. It is better to feel confident in what you have then to rely on someone else to do the work for you. Be sure to pay attention to expiry dates on kits, as some will have expiry dates. You will need to include them in your rotation and inspection so that you can replace anything that expires.

Task 33: GnG Bag for Mild Emergency

Your GnG bag for mild emergencies should be full of everything you would need in an emergency at home or close to home. The bag should contain everything you would need in a mild emergency. Your A-Team contact sheet, water, prevention checklists, food, and a first aid kit should all be kept in the mild GnG bag.

Keeping everything in a GnG bag, even if it will only be used at home, means that you can quickly grab it and bring it to the scene of an emergency and promptly use anything you need. You can also keep this bag near your moderate to extreme GnG bag as you will want to take it with you in a moderate or extreme situation, too.

Task 34: GnG Bag for Moderate to Extreme Emergency

Your moderate to extreme emergency GnG bag should contain absolutely everything you would need to survive any emergency. This includes all of your Bushcraft gear, plus everything you would need for food, water, shelter, fire, and first aid in a moderate to extreme emergency situation. These should be kept next to your GnG bag for mild situations so that you can grab all of your GnG bags and get out as soon as you can. Make sure all of your GnG bags are easily accessible, well-stocked, and organized in a way that makes it easy for you to access anything you may need in any situation you may happen upon.

CHAPTER 6

How To Leave An Urban Environment

Leaving an urban environment may sound easy in theory, but the reality is that if you are going to survive after you leave, you are going to have to know what you are doing. Urban living is much different from rural living, and even more different from living in the wilderness. Be ready to not only access your survival environment but to navigate it as well.

There are five things you must do if you are going to safely leave an urban environment and successfully survive in a rural or wilderness environment. These include: preparing your supplies, plotting your destination, educating yourself on your destination, learning skills ahead of time, and securing the first 5 of survival.

Preparing Your Supplies

Before you ever leave your urban environment, you will first need to prepare your supplies. Have your GnG bags packed, survival vest available, and everything ready to go at all times. In an urban environment, you have far greater access to the tools, supplies, and resources that you will need to survive in the bush, so you will want to collect these before leaving.

Moderate to extreme emergencies that require you to leave urban environments often make it so that you are unable to access supplies, as well. For example, a hurricane would shut down all of the grocery stores and gas stations in your area as everyone runs to protect themselves. Do not wait until an emergency strikes to prepare these supplies. Otherwise, you will find yourself struggling to get anything at all. Supplies may become inaccessible, they will sell out quickly, and accessing them even if they are available could become dangerous. Further, having to stop to get supplies first wastes your precious time that could instead be spent getting away to your BOHS location. Having them on hand is the only sure way to ensure that you have what you need and that you can escape to safety as quickly as possible.

Again, always check your supplies every 6-12 months and never leave supplies wiped out. If you use anything out of your first aid kit, for example, make sure you promptly replace it. Or, if you find yourself using things regularly, such as bandages, keep a different box for the house and a separate pack for the GnG bag. That way, you always have some on hand in your emergency bag. This is the only way to ensure that when you find yourself in an emergency, you have everything you need available for you right away.

Plotting Your Destination

You should never leave an urban environment without first knowing where you are going. Having a BOHS identified in advance ensures that you know exactly where to head in case of a moderate to extreme emergency situation. Driving aimlessly out of the city with no clear destination is a sure way to find yourself in potentially even more of a dangerous situation than you were already in.

Even during every day settings, the safest driving technique is to go directly from route A to route B. Naturally, the less time spent on the road, the less you are endangered by your moving vehicle or other moving vehicles. Now let's consider an emergency situation. In an emergency situation, no matter how level-headed you tend to be, you are going to be under stress. Further, there is no way to know whether or not the road to safety is available, or if any of your backup routes are accessible, either. Ultimately, you are hopeful that you are heading to safety, but you may still run into troubles along the way. If you do not know where you are going, you increase the amount of time you spend on a potentially dangerous road that you are unfamiliar with. This can also increase your stress levels, making driving even more dangerous.

You should always identify your BOHS location in advance and have a secondary BOHS location available in case the first one does not work out. This way, you can feel confident that you know where you are going and how to get there. There is no increased risk of you being on the road too long, or heading to a location you are not familiar with.

Educating Yourself on Your Destination

Beyond knowing what your specific destination is, you also need to educate yourself on your specific destination. Educate yourself on everything that would be relevant to you surviving in this location, *and* get out there and see it for yourself. Surviving on assumptions is never a good idea; you want certainty and confidence in your survival situation.

While educating yourself on your BOHS destination, start by educating yourself on exactly how to get there. Look for a direct route, as well as alternate routes. Then, educate yourself on what methods will be required for you to get to that location. Will you be able to drive straight in? Or are you going to have to park your car lower down and walk into the proper camping area?

You will need to educate yourself about the environment itself, too. Are you going to a space that is occupied by the desert? Wetlands? Tundra? Consider the climate, the geography, and what the terrain itself is like. How easy is it to move around in this terrain? What types of threats, dangers, or other things do you need to consider when walking in this area? Will you need to cut out paths? And if so, how will you do it? Consider everything you will need to know for getting there, setting up, and navigating the terrain as you survive in this location.

Lastly, educate yourself on the vegetation, insects, and animals in that area. What plants are you likely to come across? Take note of which plants are useful, which are edible, and which plants are dangerous. Keep a book handy, so you can educate yourself in the field, rather than trying to rely on memory when you are already stressed. Consider the insects, as well. Some insects will be harmless, but some may be dangerous. How can you protect yourself against pests to avoid being contaminated with a disease or affected by a venomous bite? Then, think about wildlife. What types of critters are you likely to come across? Which can be eaten, which can be ignored, and which are considered threats or dangers to your wellbeing?

After you have educated yourself on everything, prepare yourself to deal with it all, too. Customize your GnG bags and survival gear to suit the terrain, the vegetation, the animals, and the likely tasks you will have to engage in so that you can survive in that area. Get out in the field and actually visit that area, too, to ensure your assumptions are correct and your preparations are on par for the environment. The more prepared you are, the better your chances of survival will be.

Learning Skills In Advance

In addition to preparing your supplies in advance, you should also focus on learning skills in advance, too. At least, learn as many as you reasonably can. Educate yourself on what skills will be necessary to your survival and begin to discover how you can master those skills, even while living in an urban environment. Some you may be able to practice at home or in your urban setting, while others you may benefit from going camping in a region similar to your BOHS location, or in your BOHS location specifically. Do whatever you can to learn as much as possible beforehand so that when you arrive in the field in a survival emergency, you are safe and ready to face that emergency situation in every way possible.

Some of the skills you might consider learning in advance are in the five main areas of your survival, including water, food, shelter, fire, and first aid. Below, you will find some skills you should start focusing on developing right away.

- Water: how to find water, how to treat water, how to test the water, how to store water.

- Food: how to cook different basic recipes, how to set up a trap, how to fish, how to find bait, how to track animals, how to preserve animals, how to forage, how to identify edible plants from toxic plants, how to store food safely in a campsite.
- Shelter: how to build a tent, how to make a tent out of a tarp, how to make a shelter out of all natural items (branches, brush, leaves, grasses, etc.), how to insulate a shelter, how to check the environment for a safe location to build a shelter.
- Fire: how to identify different pieces of wood, how to locate wood, how to cut wood, how to split wood, how to make a basic fire lay, how to make a fire starter, how to start a fire, how to fuel a fire, how to safely cook over a fire.
- First aid: how to pack a first aid kit, how to use the different elements of a first aid kit, how to dress a wound, how to treat a burn, how to treat gastrointestinal issues, local plants with medicinal values, how to make a poultice, how to set a bone, how to transport someone who is unable to move, how to resuscitate someone.

Securing the First 5 of Survival

The first five of survival include water, food, shelter, fire, and first aid or safety. These are used to help secure your core temperature and provide you with everything you need in order to survive. If you set yourself up well, they are also set up in a way that amplifies your comfort and convenience, which makes survival a lot easier. In an urban setting, you are likely already educated on how to secure these five elements of your wellbeing. In an off-grid survival situation, these five elements change a bit, though.

Water is not fetched from a tap or a store, but instead from a water source. You need to be prepared to locate a water source, carry water back to camp, treat the water, and drink it. Store water in stainless steel containers that have been sterilized in boiling water and cooled completely to avoid burning yourself.

Food is not fetched from a store, either. You are going to need to be able to track food sources and trap or fish for those sources so that you can bring meat back to camp. Protein and fat are essential staples of a survivalists diet as it provides you with the best energy to keep you going. Most of your calories are burnt when resting, so when you are in a situation where you need to take action, you will *definitely* need to prepare yourself by bulking up on as much protein and fat as possible. You also need to learn how to safely forage for food, clean food, and consume food from plant life in the local area.

Shelter is not put in place, nor can you hire a building crew to build your shelter. You are going to need to know how to fly a tarp, how to set up a tent, how to build a shelter, and where to build a shelter. You are also going to need to know how to make sure that the shelter is waterproof and warm so that you do not risk yourself by remaining too wet or by cooling down too much on cooler days or nights.

Fire is not something that can easily be created through candles, fireplaces, gas ranges, or barbecues when you are surviving in the woods. You need to know how to make a fire lay, start a fire, and maintain a fire. You are also going to need to know how to safely cook on the fire so that you do not burn yourself, but you can consume the food you have harvested safely.

Lastly, backwoods first aid is different from urban first aid because you do not have immediate access to trained medical staff or sterilized medical equipment that can be used in any emergency or first aid situation. Even if you are in a situation where you can call the authorities for assistance, there is no guarantee that they will get there in time. You will need to know how to treat all minor injuries and illnesses and how to address all major injuries and illnesses until you can get the help of a medical professional. If you have escaped to live off-grid because authorities are a danger to you and your family, you might have to learn to do even more first aid so you can adequately deal with emergencies in the bush, without help.

Practice Evacuations

Everything always works perfectly in theories. In practical application is where you begin to run into trouble with any plans you may have prepared for yourself and your family. An essential step to preparing yourself to leave an urban environment is practicing your evacuation ahead of time when no pressing emergency is present. Practice evacuations ensure that you have a concise and realistic understanding of what is required during a real evacuation and allows you to create an evacuation protocol that actually works.

Ensure that your household and any other households involved in your A-Team practice evacuations every so often to ensure you are all prepared for a real evacuation, should one be required. It may feel silly to practice escaping when no threat is looming, but understand that this critical step can help you recognize weaknesses in your plan and offset them with plan adjustments ahead of time. This way, during a real threat, your evacuation plan works, and everyone safely arrives at your ERP, or IRP, depending on the type of evacuation being practiced.

An effective way to practice an evacuation would be to first compose a theory of how your evacuation should look. Then, create a theoretical emergency and form a "sudden call" to the A-Team of this emergency. Immediately, everyone should enact the evacuation protocol and begin fulfilling their role in that protocol. The practice drill is over when everyone meets at the ERP or the IRP, depending on the drill being practiced. Immediately after, everyone should reflect on how the practice drill went, and what could have improved the quality of the evacuation. Attempt to imagine additional challenges that may have been imposed due to emergencies, as well, to get a clearer understanding of how safety during the evacuation can be secured. Practice your adjusted drill until you have reached the point where you have an evacuation protocol that works.

Practice your final evacuation protocol at least once per year once it has been finalized. This ensures that as things change, such as someone moves, someone is no longer physically capable, or new people join the A-Team; these changes are accommodated for in your evacuation protocol. Adequate, up-to-date preparedness will always ensure the smoothest possible escape from a dangerous emergency at any given time, so take this step seriously and practice it frequently.

CHAPTER 7

Long Term Off-Grid Survival

If you find yourself needing to survive off-grid for a long time, you are going to need to acquire additional skills that will allow you to secure your survival for extended periods. Knowing what no respite is coming and that you have to fend for yourself for extended periods can be frightening. Still, it is entirely possible and can be done successfully. As long as you are prepared to learn the necessary skills and implement the required steps, a human can survive through just about anything.

Foraging and Scavenging In Natural Environments

Procuring food in natural environments is not always easy, but it is necessary. You cannot live solely off of game meat for survival, especially over long periods of time, as you expose yourself to many different types of illnesses. Humans require a number of vitamins that come from plant matter to be able to maintain a healthy immune system, which will, in turn, fend off any illness and help with faster healing.

Foraging and scavenging in natural environments depend on what environment you are living in. If you are living long term, you are going to want to have enough food available to help you through periods where food may be more challenging to get. For example, in most areas, winters are particularly challenging because they are cooler, and many animals stop reproducing, go into hibernation, and generally lay low for the season. As well, hunting in winter seasons is more challenging because of the snow and the cold. Having a regular system for foraging, scavenging, and hunting will ensure that you have enough food to last you.

Raised Bed Gardening

One way you can secure food for yourself, and the A-Team is to engage in raised bed gardening. Raised bed gardening can be done at home or off-grid and can be incredibly helpful in keeping enough food available for you and your family. When it comes to raised bed gardening, you need to think about growing hardy crops that are going to get you the furthest and that are able to handle harsher growing conditions. This way, if you have a rough growing season, you are still likely to get some food out of it. You should also grow foods that preserve well as it is unlikely that you will be able to consume all that food at once. Further, it would be unwise of you to grow plenty of food only to have none of it last through until the end of winter.

Another thing you are going to have to consider with raised bed gardening is the element of competition. Pests such as insects, rodents, birds, small mammals, and even some medium and large mammals can come through and destroy any crop in a matter of hours. You need to have a method in place for protecting your crop, while also having a method in place for harvesting fresh produce before anyone else gets to it. I talk more about the specifics of raised bed gardening in *Survival 101: Raised Bed Gardening*.

Long Term Food Preservation

Long term food preservation will ensure that you always have an abundance of food, even during seasons where gathering food may be more challenging. There are many different methods of long term food preservation, all of which can be useful in preserving your harvest through slow seasons. Canning is perhaps the most popular method of preservation when it comes to things like fruits and vegetables. However, your ability to can will depend on whether or not you were able to bring any canning supplies with you. If you can, have a proper canning guide on hand, too. A proper book will educate you on how to safely can all of your supplies to avoid accidental illness or death due to botulism.

Drying out and dehydrating fruit and vegetables is another great way to preserve your harvest. This can be done with minimal equipment, and the food can be consumed dry or rehydrated at a later point with filtered water when you are cooking.

Drying, salting, and smoking meat are all the best methods for preserving meat when you are in the wilderness. These methods will ensure that your meat is safe so that you can consume it at a later date. I discuss more food preservation in *Survival 101: Food Storage*.

Preparing for Climate Changes

If you are going to be surviving in the wilderness for an extended period, you are going to need to know how to prepare for climate change. The general way the seasons of survival in the wilderness go include: spring – start the harvest, summer, – grow the harvest, fall – preserve the harvest, and winter, – consume the harvest. You will need to prepare in other ways, too. For summer, you will want to prepare for animals awakening, bugs becoming more active, and more bacteria and viruses waking up. In the winter, you want to prepare for how much more challenging it will be for you to access food and water sources by having plenty on hand for you to consume.

You will also want to prepare your shelter for climate change. In the summer, you will want to do what you can to keep your shelter cooler so that you do not overheat in it, while during winter months, you are going to want to insulate your shelter so that you stay warmer.

Building Long Term Shelter

Long term shelter is going to be necessary if you are going to be surviving somewhere for a lengthy period. While tarp shelters and tents are great for short term survival, they will not suffice if you need to be anywhere for a longer period. Over longer periods, these shelters become a risk because they are able to tear, they are not as easy to keep warm, and they do not do a particularly good job at keeping predators and pests out. Building long term shelter will ensure that you have everything you need to keep yourself safe and healthy for long periods.

Long term shelter should consider longevity, security, and all of your fundamental needs. It should be built in a way that is lasting, that keeps animals out to the best of your ability, and that makes doing things like storing your goods, cooking, and doing other such things much easier. You may want to build a long term sleeping cabin, as well as a food cabin and a storage cabin a ways away from your sleeping cabin. This way, you can safely protect all of your belongings while still following proper practice to protect yourself, too.

Navigating Disasters

Navigating disasters in the wilderness may seem challenging. Things like financial collapses will not affect your living in the wilderness; however, they may drive you there. Preparing for a financial collapse is best done by storing as much as you possibly can, and learning how to grow and harvest more so that you can rely on yourself for subsistence. This way, if the financial collapse occurs and money becomes worthless, you can still protect your survival. Another situation that may completely block you from being able to access what you need would be offense warfare attacks. Some places are prone to attacks by opposing armies or by civil armies in the case of civil warfare. In these circumstances, if you go off-grid, you want to stay in hiding to avoid anyone infiltrating you and destroying your survival situation.

Pandemics are tough to deal with. Early on, you may have access to all of your normal supply chains, but as pandemics, rage on it can become increasingly more dangerous to live in an urban environment and interact with other people. Moving your A-Team away to an off-grid situation and avoiding or eliminating contact with the outside world is a great way to prevent yourself and the A-Team from contracting the pandemic virus. Many believe that an illness may one day come through and wipe out civilization, which is why they prepare, and these individuals live as off-grid as possible to avoid coming into contact with any such pandemics, and ultimately dying.

Natural disasters can lead to short and long term survival situations. When they involve financial collapse, for example, they end up becoming long term survival situations. Regardless of how your home may come back together, the recession it leaves your region in can be devastating. In a natural disaster, you should be aware of how the disaster affects your home, your travel route, and your BOHS location. Act accordingly. If it is unsafe for you to stay home or go to the BOHS location, rely on an alternate plan to protect yourself and the A-Team.

The best way to navigate disasters is to plan for them and to create a clear plan for how you will deal with any such disaster. You should also have back up plans for what you are going to do if your ideal plans do not turn out. As well, you should educate yourself on what it is like to attempt to survive such a disaster so that you are prepared for what may be expected of you in order for survival to even be possible. Always plan and prepare for the worst in survival situations, so you have everything you need to survive anything that happens to you. That way, you always have the best chance of survival.

CHAPTER 8

Emergency And First Aid

Dealing with emergencies and first aid situations in the bush can be scary. In some cases, it may be possible for you to deal with them yourself. With others, you may need to contact support to assist you with the situation you have found yourself in. There are some general guidelines you should follow to help you make your judgment call. Still, at the end of the day, you are going to need to decide what is right for the situation you are in and go from there.

When to Contact the Police

In mild emergencies, contacting the police or your local emergency line is a great way to get access to help. In moderate to extreme emergencies, calling the police should be something you do only if you need to. The reason behind this is that you do not want to contact the police and overburden their system with calls from a local emergency. Alternatively, you do not wish to contact the police and rely on them if they are going to be a danger to you or your family.

More recently, the threat of places turning into a police state has become more significant than ever. That threat means that not everyone can rely on the local police force. When a police state is enacted, none of us may be able to genuinely rely on the police force because it operates on a different agenda. Trusting in them could lead to imprisonment or even death in some cases. If you are in a situation where you have escaped from a police state or where you are likely to be harmed by the police, you should refrain from calling the cops and instead have a support group of people you can call on for assistance in emergencies. This counts whether you are still in urban civilization, or if you have evacuated to the bush to survive off-grid due to an emergency you may be facing.

When to Contact FEMA

FEMA, or the Federal Emergency Management Agency, is located in the Department of Homeland Security. They are responsible for coordinating the federal government's response to natural and man-made disasters. In some situations, FEMA can be incredibly helpful with a disaster you may be facing. FEMA can also help deal with acts of terror, allowing them to provide a great deal of support to anyone who may be facing a disaster.

You should only contact FEMA if you have faced an emergency, and if you feel confident, they can help. If, however, you are someone who is likely to be questioned or imprisoned by the government, calling FEMA may not be a good idea. At times, particularly when a police state is enacted, relying on any government infrastructure may be dangerous. If you have any reason to believe you would be put at risk, avoid relying on FEMA, and instead navigate the disaster using your own survival skills and supplies.

Utilizing Government Infrastructure

Relying on government infrastructure is something that you need to consider, particularly when there is a great deal of mistrust in the government deeply. At this time, as we face challenges with the coronavirus pandemic, many people do not trust the government and fear what may happen if they do. This can make trusting government infrastructure fearsome, especially if you believe they are intentionally engaging in wrongdoings.

Ultimately, if you are in an emergency where you believe the government themselves are unreliable and are a threat, you need to use your best judgment and avoid infrastructure at all costs. Do everything you can to survive on your own, and only call for support or rely on government infrastructure if there is absolutely no other chance. Even then, do so in a way that minimizes the risk of you and everyone you are surviving with. For example, if you are in a situation where you are surviving off-grid to avoid a police state, but someone in your camp is extremely hurt, you should bring that person down into civility and contact support for them. Then, to the best of your ability, get away from that location, and let them get help. This way, anyone who may need it can access support, but the rest of the A-Team remains safe and away from the risk of being found or harmed.

If there is no police state enacted, and there is no overarching reason to believe the government is a direct threat to you, use your best judgment. Always do what you can to only use government infrastructure when it is required, and do your best to rely on yourself and the A-Team as much as possible. This keeps you out of the government's crosshairs and in a safer position to protect yourself and other members of the A-Team.

First Aid Methods You Should Know

One of the best ways you can protect the A-Team and minimize reliance on government infrastructure is to learn how to treat minor things yourself at home or at the BOHS location. These basic first aid methods ensure that you are able to treat minor conditions in people so that they do not have to rely on government infrastructure. If treated effectively, their condition should improve, and you should be able to keep them out of the system. The three things you should know how to do on the field include dressing a wound, treating gastrointestinal illness, and dealing with broken bones.

Dressing a Wound

To dress a wound, start by cleansing the wound using an antiseptic cleaner, which will sterilize the wound from any bacteria that may have broken the skin barrier. If the injury is deep enough, you will need to sew it together using a sterile needle and medical thread. Next, you should use medical glue, medical tape, or pine resin in a pinch, to "glue" the wound together, especially if it is an unusually large wound. Even smaller wounds can use these to create a protective barrier between the injury and the external world, while the wound itself is healing. Once done, you should place clean gauze over the wound and secure it in place. Then, prevent the wound from being rubbed or aggravated by any external sources. Replace the dressing every 4-6 hours to avoid bacteria getting into the wound and causing illness through the wound itself.

Treating a Gastrointestinal Illness

A gastrointestinal illness may be bothersome in an urban environment, but in a survival environment, they can be fatal. Treating them promptly avoids someone becoming dehydrated or malnourished and ensures that they have a better chance of survival. Start by making sure that the affected person has access to clean water and high-quality protein. Sipping water and slowly snacking on dried meat is a great way to keep them hydrated and nourished. Next, you should use medicine to help treat the gastrointestinal illness. If you have any medicine on hand, use that. Otherwise, use the inner bark from a sassafras tree or a white oak tree to make a tea and consume that to treat any gastrointestinal illnesses. If sassafras or white oak do not grow in your area, educate yourself on alternative remedies that you can locate in your region's natural flora. Use this knowledge to improvised based on your current location.

Dealing With a Broken Bone

Broken bones can be incredibly dangerous in a wilderness survival location. The scent of blood from the wound can attract wildlife, and the bone itself can make saving yourself far more challenging. If a bone is completely broken or protruding, the only thing you can do is wrap the injury with a soft padded blanket and get that person to trained medical staff as soon as possible.

If a bone is fractured but not completely broken and has not broken surface, you may be able to deal with it at camp. For digits, for example, you can wrap them against a small branch so that the branch holds them straight and steady while they are healing. For legs, a larger branch can be secured to the limb to encourage the limb to heal. The limb should also be carefully wrapped to keep it protected. There should be plenty of protection between the limb and the branch to avoid wounds from rubbing. If it is an arm that is broken, a splint may be the best option for healing the broken arm. You could also attach a branch to the arm to keep it straight and sturdy, again keeping plenty of padding between the arm and the branch to avoid wounds from rubbing.

CONCLUSION

Surviving a dangerous situation seems like a nightmare. For most people, they will never actually have to live through it. For many, however, emergencies strike and lead to them having to protect themselves and fend for themselves. This may only be for the foreseeable future, or for the long haul, depending on the type of disaster they have found themselves in.

The thing about emergencies is that we never expect them, and if we do, we never expect them to be *that* bad. When they do strike, however, they can rapidly catch us off guard and leave us in a do-or-die situation. The only way to protect yourself against emergencies entails assuming that you will inevitably face one at some point in your life and prepare accordingly. You can do this by preparing yourself for mild, moderate, and extreme emergencies. If anything does happen, you are fully equipped.

As you continue to prepare for emergencies, I encourage you to keep *Survival 101: Beginner's Guide 2020* available for you to access at all times. Use this book to help you review your 34 tasks and run your rotation and inspection checklist. As well, use it to help guide you through the tasks that you may need to enact if and when you find yourself in an emergency setting. It is important that you assume that any stress you face during an emergency will disrupt your memory. Keeping clear guides on what to do ensures that should this happen, you have everything you need to stay focused and survive. Having this book printed and available in your GnG bag helps. I also encourage you to keep printed copies of *Survival 101: Bushcraft, Survival 101: Food Storage,* and *Survival 101: Raised Bed Gardening for Beginners* on hand. All four of these books will serve you massively if you ever find yourself in a survival situation.

Don't stop here, either. Continue educating yourself on what it takes to survive. Study your local environment, learn new skills, and prepare yourself in a hands-on way so that if and when you find yourself in this situation, you are ready. When it comes to your survival, you are ultimately responsible. While urban environments may be comfortable, avoid becoming complacent. Not educating yourself on survival techniques is foolish and dangerous, and can ultimately lead to illness, injuries, or fatalities during an emergency.

Before you go, I want to ask one favor. If you could please review *Survival 101: Beginner's Guide 2020* on Amazon Kindle, I would greatly appreciate it. Your honest review will help others discover this great title, while also helping me create more great titles for you.

Thank you, and best of luck! Stay safe out there.

DESCRIPTION

Do you know how to survive without access to modern supply chains?

If you had to evacuate your town immediately, would you feel confident in your ability to survive?

Are you aware of the 34 tasks required for you to survive any situation you are faced with?

The state of the modern world has many people questioning their safety and wondering what they would do if faced with a survival situation. A global pandemic has left many realizing that survival is not as easy as going to the store for your necessities.

Our modern world has made survival easy for us, but it has also made us complacent. Being able to go to the grocery store for food, turn on the tap for water, and turn up the heat for warmth means that many of us do not know how to survive without these luxuries. While they may seem basic to you, the reality is that they can all be taken away in a matter of minutes. What then?

The wakeup call we are all facing means that every one of us could stand to learn more about how to manage our survival. After all, our survival relies *on us individually*. That is why I comprised a series of Survival 101 books designed to help you survive any situation, including this one. *Survival 101: Beginner's Guide 2020* will help you get started with managing your own survival no matter where you are at right now so that you can feel a sense of security in your ability to adapt and overcome.

Some of what you will learn in *Survival 101: Beginner's Guide 2020* includes:

- How you can prepare for any survival situation

- Key terms you should know about when reading survival manuals

- The first five things you have to secure to ensure your survival

- An overview of the survival task list

- A detailed description and guide for each of the 34 tasks, including how to prepare for them and how to enact them in an emergency

- How to safely and properly leave an urban environment

- How to secure your long term survival in an off-grid situation

- What to do in case of an emergency, and who to call (if anyone)

- Detailed guides on what to do in certain first aid settings

- Checklists and detailed lists of what should be included in your survival gear

- And more!

Now more than ever, you need to know how to protect your survival and the survival of the people you love. Although our modern systems may be nice, they are not sustainable in an emergency, and in those situations, you need to know what to do in order to live through them. Buy *Survival 101: Beginner's Guide 2020* today and discover what you need to do in order to survive any emergency you may come across. You can't afford to wait any longer!

www.ingramcontent.com/pod-product-compliance
Lightning Source LLC
Chambersburg PA
CBHW081753100526
44592CB00015B/2418